THE WAY OF

MASTERY

≈≪ BOOK ONE ≫≈

THE WAY OF THE HEART

SHANTI CHRISTO FOUNDATION

~ Dedication ~

This book is dedicated to our beloved friend Rex Schirmer, whose devotion to Truth and Love has inspired and uplifted the Shanti Christo Foundation for many years.

We are deeply grateful for his generous contributions and wise guidance.

Discernment vs Judgement

Copyright © 2009, 2013
by Shanti Christo Foundation

First Printing 2009
Second Printing 2014

All rights reserved. No part of this book may be reproduced in any form by any electronic or mechanical means including information storage and retrieval systems without permission in writing from the publisher.

Published by
Shanti Christo Foundation

ISBN 978-0-9771632-6-7
Library of Congress Catalog Card Number 2009910302
Manufactured in the United States of America

CONTENTS

Introduction VI
The promise VIII

Book One – The Way of the Heart

Lesson 1: The Way That Calls You Home 2
   The First Step in Awakening   9
   The Way of the Heart Calls You Home   19

Lesson 2: You Create Your Experience 24
   What You Perceive Is Communicated Always   25
   Peace Flows from Alignment with the Mind of God   30
   Mastery Arises from Innocence   38
   What You Decree, Is   40
   Practicing the First Two Axioms   46
   Exercise in Conscious Creation   48

Lesson 3: The Power of Forgiveness 53
   Forgiveness, the Bridge to the Soul of Your Brother and Sister   61
   The Veil of Projection   63
   Awakening Requires Vigilance and Discipline   66
   How Forgiveness Heals   74
   Reactivity Indicates the Need for Self Forgiveness   80
   Healing Exercise   88
   Ending Your Day   87

LESSON 4: FOLLOWING THE THREAD OF DESIRE........92
  Desire Is Everything   99
  Releasing Judgment of Desire   106
  Desire Links You to the Will of God   111
  An Exercise in Trusting Desire   117

LESSON 5: THE KEYS TO THE KINGDOM..................128
  The First Key Is Desire   134
  The Second Key Is Intention   135
  The Third Key Is Allowance   138
  The Fourth Key Is Surrender   144
  The Importance of Humility   148

LESSON 6: LOVE HEALS ALL THINGS......................161
  If You Would Know Love, Know Your Self   164
  The Primary Characteristic of Mastery   168
  All You Need Is Love   174
  Feeling Is the Doorway to Love and Freedom   180
  Only Through Feeling Do You Awaken   188

LESSON 7: BIRTHING THE MIND OF CHRIST............191
  The Shadow of Fear   200
  Birthing the Christ Mind   205

LESSON 8: DROPPING PEBBLES INTO THE
POOL OF AWARENESS 214
  You Only Experience What You Have
  Chosen to Create   220
  You Are Not a Victim of the World You See   226

Creating as Christ 229

Creating Mastery 234

Lesson 9: All Events Are Neutral ... 244

Look with Innocence on What You Value 251

The Power of Your Thoughts 258

Five Minutes a Day — The Foundation of Mastery 263

Planting the Seed that Produces the Desired Result 272

Lesson 10: The Way Is Easy and Without Effort ... 280

Acknowledge the Truth That Sets You Free 286

Commit to Awakening to the Peace Already Within You 291

Recognizing the Presence of Christ Within 298

A Simple Practice 302

Celebrate Your Re-birth as Christ 305

Lesson 11: A Meditation Into the Heart of Christ ... 309

Here Is the Place of Certainty, Power and Fulfillment 314

Lesson 12: Receive the Pearls of Grace ... 327

Discover the Obstacles to Love 329

A Meditation of Release 336

Call for Assistance to Dissolve Fears 347

INTRODUCTION

You hold in your hands the treasured teachings of Jeshua ben Joseph (Jesus), one of the greatest *Masters* humankind has ever known. These teachings were given during the years 1994-1997. Please do not hurry as you read through each lesson. Rather, allow each sentence to be held within the heart, each idea to fill the mind and the body with its very real frequency or vibration. For each word, the structure of each sentence, the cadence and the humor, is by design.

These words are to be studied and savored over and over, until their meaning deepens and flowers into the grace of Christ living in you and as you, allowing the ray of that Light to penetrate your mind, correcting every perception you have ever held about yourself or the world. You will then find your gifts being formulated in new ways. You will find that you have an unseen Teacher revealing to you what you are ready to learn. And your life will begin to be guided by a Voice that is not your own until the voice you have called your own is no longer heard. And the mind will know perfect peace.

Does this take time? You are as close as the choice to teach only Love. The 12 lessons contained in this volume reveal that "Way" taught to Jeshua Himself, and now lovingly presented by Him for you, so that the choice for Love becomes your every thought, your every breath, your every action extended to the world as the awakened Christ.

May you be transformed by *The Way of the Heart* in your unique process of remembering who you really are.

I promise you this...

If you become wholly committed to awakening from the dream you have dreamt since the stars first began to appear in the heavens and if your one desire is to be only what God created, then lay at the altar of your heart with every breath, everything you think you know, everything you think you need, and look lovingly upon every place that fear has made a home in your mind, and allow correction to come. It will come. Regardless of how you experience it, it will come. And the day and the moment will arise and all of your pain and fear and suffering will have vanished like a wind that pushes the foam of the wave away, revealing the clarity of the ocean beneath you. You will literally feel throughout your being that there never was a dream. Some memories might remain with you and you will know that somewhere you must have dreamt a dream or had a thought of wondering what it would be like to be other than the way God

I promise you this...

created you, but it will be such a faint echo that it will leave no trace upon you. In your heart you will smile gently regardless of the circumstances in which you find yourself. There will be peace from the crown of the head to the tips of the toes, and that peace will walk before you wherever you go. It will enter a room before you enter it with a body, and those who are becoming sensitive will wonder who has come into their place. And some will even say, "Behold, I believe Christ has come for dinner." And you will be that One, for that is who you are — Christ eternal.

~Jeshua

BOOK ONE

THE WAY OF THE HEART

Lesson 1

The Way That Calls You Home

Now, we begin.

Beloved friends, I come forth to abide with you where you believe yourself to be. I come not for myself, but for you. I come not to teach you, but to love you until you choose from the depth within your own being to set aside every illusion you have ever given credence to, and to remember the Truth which alone is true.

For indeed in that hour, there is a transcendence of all that knows limitation. There is a transcendence of all that knows coming and going, birth and death. There is but the Mind of Christ within which each of us—as a spark of divine light, as a sunbeam to the sun—rests eternally in perfect communion and communication always.

The great secret is this is the state of your reality. In each and every moment, you abide in perfect

Lesson 1: *The Way That Calls You Home*

communion with the whole of creation since all things are but temporary modifications of the one fundamental energy that I have chosen to call the Christ Mind, the offspring of the Father.

Beloved friends, I come to where you choose to be. And if you would choose to open that place within the heart and within the mind in which you can communicate with me directly, I will meet you there as well.

What is important then, by way of beginning, is to consider this simple fact: Your experience is always the effect of where you choose to focus the attention of your consciousness, itself being unlimited forever, embracing all the many dimensions of creation. You abide in that which embraces all things, in all ways, and at all times. In truth, you do not know separation, birth or death, gain or loss.

As you focus your attention on reading these words, recognize how you, as an infinite being, have deliberately chosen to participate in a form of experience. You will read words that carry certain meanings for each of you. And you each will color that meaning according to the perceptions that *you* have chosen to place value upon.

Does this mean that some are ahead and some behind? It only seems that way. In reality, each of you is equal. Each of you chooses from your infinite freedom to attract to yourself certain vibrational frequencies, certain forms or qualities of experience. That freedom is what you abide in *always,* from before the foundations of this world and long after this world ceases to be.

In each and every moment, you cannot be a victim of what you see, and nothing is outside of you. What you experience you have directly and deliberately called to yourself. If you hold the thought, "I do not like what I have called to myself," that is perfectly fine. For you have called to yourself the experience of being in judgment of yourself. Merely look with the wonder of a child and see what it feels like and ask yourself, "Is this an energy I wish to continue in or would I choose something else?"

For ultimately, when all possible choices within the dream of separation have been made, have been tasted, have been felt and have been known, finally there emerges the still, quiet voice of Spirit that

LESSON 1: *The Way That Calls You Home*

speaks through the soul, whispering of the one Truth, the one Reality, the one Love, the one peace and the one bliss that is continual.

Then the soul begins to turn from the things of this created world. It begins to withdraw its attention from its attachments to all of the things it has called to itself. It begins to transcend its sense of identification with the vibrational frequencies it had only meant to play with, and then took seriously. It is seriousness within the mind that is the creation of ego. And it is great seriousness that holds the vibrations of what you would no longer choose to experience within the field of your being, within the field of your soul.

As you as the soul—the individual divine spark—begin to choose to withdraw the attention and the value you have placed upon all things, as you learn to simplify the nature of your own consciousness, as you realize that you can surrender into something that seems beyond you and that you can entertain the insane thought of trusting the invisible, you come more and more to be less and less.

As you become less and less of what you thought

you were, conversely, you become more and more of what your Father created you to be—the thought of perfect Love in form, a channel, a simple vehicle through which the Love of Spirit can shine forth. Your only task becomes the cleaning of your windows, the polishing of your floors and the weeding of your garden so that that Light can pour forth unimpeded.

No longer will you find the need to defend perceptions you had identified with in error. You will indeed know when you have come to that state of awakening. For you will be able to look upon all created things that you have ever experienced, all reactions you have ever held within the mind, all perceptions, all judgments, all desires that you have ever held for anyone or anything. And as they arise in your mind, they will not disturb your peace.

And you will smile. You will see that within your consciousness have arisen all saintliness and all devilishness. You have been both saint and sinner. And your happiness and your unhappiness have been merely an effect of where you chose to place your attention.

LESSON 1: *The Way That Calls You Home*

Indeed beloved friends, I come forth to meet you wherever you are because I have chosen to use the infinite power of consciousness given me of the Father—as equally as it is given unto you—to discover how deep delight can be when the mind is focused only on seeing from, and seeing only, the Mind of Christ. I have, therefore, called to myself all multitude of experiences—even when I walked upon your beloved Earth as a man—to challenge myself, to test myself, to condition myself to rise above, to transcend all possible experiences that could distract me from the remembrance of who I am.

By the way, my crucifixion was simply the climax of my own direct choice to be challenged by the events of space and time so that I could cultivate within myself the ability to see from, and to see only, the perfect purity of the Mind of Christ.

The point I am trying to make with you is that in each and every moment, what you are experiencing in the realm of your emotions and mind, and the effects—to a latter degree—within the body are there because you, from your infinite freedom, have simply *selected* that experience to focus your attention on so that you can see what the effects are.

The insanity does not come from having chosen to see something other than the Mind of Christ. The insanity that you experience as your pain, your suffering, your seeking and your dramas comes only from your mistaken choice to become *identified* with what arises in the field of your awareness. You, therefore, lose the sight of innocence. For all events are perfectly neutral, and you are free to see them any way you want.

When a child is born—and many of you who are mothers know this—you can experience a depth of joy that is unspeakable. Likewise, you can also experience fear and contraction at the thought of having to be responsible for a child. When a loved one dies and you experience grief and suffering, rest assured it is because you have chosen to contract your attention. Then all you can see is the loss of an animated body and thereby convince yourself that you have become separated from the loved one.

I speak from experience that separation *is* an illusion. When death occurs in your plane, in that very moment you still have the power to choose to recognize that something has changed, and to shift your attention to a different faculty that the

Lesson 1: *The Way That Calls You Home*

body could never possibly contain. One in which you perceive and hear and communicate with that spark of divine light—the soul—that seems to have given up the idea of trying to keep a physical form animated. This is imperative. In fact, it is the very first step of The Way of the Heart.

The First Step in Awakening

The first step in awakening is to allow into the mind this axiom of truth:

> Nothing that you experience is caused
> by anything outside of you.
> You experience only the effects of
> your own choice.

During the first part of this course, we will be building lesson by lesson on what I am choosing to call The Way of the Heart. It is the way unknown to the world. It is a way unknown to many that would call themselves spiritual teachers. For it is not a way of resting on or becoming dependent on magical means.

It is, rather, that pathway which cultivates within you the decision to turn your attention upon your own mind, upon your own behavior, upon what is true and real for you moment to moment. To study it, to consider it, to feel it, to breathe the light of Spirit through it, and to constantly retrain the mind so that it assumes complete responsibility in each moment.

Why is this necessary? Because without it, there can be no peace. Without it, you cannot transcend the false identifications that you have chosen. You need to come to the point where you say to yourself, "I have done this to myself. I did it; I must correct it. No one is to blame. The world is innocent."

In the lessons that follow, we will be communicating with you more and more deeply the finer points of The Way of the Heart. For it is that way that was taught to me. It is that way that brings about the reversal of every thought you have ever had about anyone or anything. It is that way, alone, which allows you to pass back through the eye of the needle, and to come to rest in the perfect peace from which you have sprung forth.

The Way of the Heart is not the way of the intellect. For indeed that aspect of the mind was never

Lesson 1: *The Way That Calls You Home*

designed to be your master. It was designed to be the humble, and—if you will pardon the expression—very stupid servant of the awakened heart.

The heart is that which feels all things, embraces all things, trusts all things, and allows all things. The heart is that in which the soul rests eternally. The heart is that which is beyond space and time and is that spark of light in the Mind of God, which is called Christ. Only in that will you find the peace that you seek.

You will discover that the pathway of awakening is not a pathway of avoidance, but a pathway of truthfulness. It is not a pathway of accomplishment and pride, but a pathway of releasing from the consciousness every hope and every wish to be special—to see yourself as having made progress—so that you can pound a fist upon the chest and spread the tail feathers. It is a transcendence of the hope of somehow getting God's attention, so that He will look upon you and say, "Oh, you have been such a good person. Yes, we will allow you into the Kingdom now."

It is a way in which you will come to cultivate—regardless of your inner experience or degree of awakening—the willingness and the art of returning to the simplicity of empty-headedness and not-knowingness with each and every breath. It is a way of life in which all things and all events become an aspect of your meditation and your prayer until there is established once again within you the Truth that is true always:

Not my will, but thine be done.

For of myself, I do nothing.

But the Father does all things through me.

Imagine then a state of being in which you walk through this world seemingly appearing like everyone else and yet, you are spacious within. You are empty within. In truth, you desire nothing, though you allow desire to move through you. And you recognize it as the voice of the Father guiding your personality, your emotions and even the body to the places, events, people and experiences through which the tapestry of the atonement—the at-one-ment—is being woven, through which all of the children of God are called home again.

You trust the complete flow of that, whether you are asked to give a speech in front of ten thou-

LESSON 1: *The Way That Calls You Home*

sand people, or you are asked to tell a friend the truth of your feelings, or whether or not you are asked to sweep the streets and live penniless. For in truth, that mind that trusts the Source of its creation allows all things, trusts all things, embraces all things and transcends all things.

Rest assured whenever you feel frustration and anxiety, it is because you have decided not to trust the Truth. And the Truth is simply this:

Only God's plan for salvation can work for you.

Your way must always fail. For your way begins with the illusory and insane assumption that you are a separate being from the Mind of God and must, therefore, direct your own course. For if you are sick and diseased and not at peace, why would you decide that you know how to create peace? It requires great humility to accept the first step of the path:

I have done all this; I must undo it.

But I have no idea how I did this.

Therefore, I must surrender to something else.

I give you this thought, and I would ask that you consider it well. What if the very life you are living, and each and every experience that is coming to you now since the moment you decided, "I have got to awaken here," was being directly sent to you of your Father because your Father knows what is necessary to unravel within your consciousness to allow you to awaken? What if the very things you are resisting are the very stepping stones to your homecoming? What if you achieved a maturity along this pathway in which you were finally willing to let things be just as they are?

If it was necessary to sweep the streets, you simply took a deep breath and said, "Father, you know the way home," and began sweeping. And up into the mind comes the thought, "Oh my god, I won't be recognized. I won't stand out. People won't think I'm special if I'm just a street sweeper." Yet you recognize, "Ah-ha, no wonder my Father wants me to do this. I've got to flush this up so that I can look at it, dis-identify from it, and learn to be the presence of Love in the sweeping of the street." In truth, I tell you the least among you—according to your perception—is already equal to the greatest. And there is none among you who is less than I am.

LESSON 1: *The Way That Calls You Home*

The Way of the Heart begins by accepting the humility that you have created quite a mess within your consciousness. You have created a labyrinth and gotten lost within it, and you do not know the way back.

It begins by accepting that of yourself, you can do nothing. For all you have managed to achieve is the creation of a whole lot of insane dramas that are occurring nowhere except within the field of your mind. They are like chimeras, like dreams. In truth, there is no difference between a waking state—in which you would be the director of your life—and the dreams you have when the body sleeps at night. They are both the same.

I wish to direct you to peace, even that peace which forever transcends the understanding and comprehension of the world. I desire—because my Father desires it through me—to bring you wholly to where I am that you might discover there is someone that got there ahead of you. And when you look closely, you will say, "Ah, it's my Self. I have always been there, but I forgot."

In the end of all journeying, in the end of all purification—and indeed purification is still necessary —you will discover that to awaken means to have journeyed nowhere. It means to have arrived at a goal that has never changed.

Awakening is only remembrance. But it is a remembrance not just of the intellect. It is not an idea, as you would understand ideas. It is an idea that vibrates through the whole field of your beingness, so that even the cells of the body—while yet the body remains coalesced together in its present form—awaken and relax into the Truth that is true always.

If you were a gardener, would you not cultivate the art of weeding your garden? Would you not look to see that the soil is just the correct dampness? Would you not keep your eye on the clouds on the horizon and the heat of the day? Would you not cover the delicate plants that need protection while they grow strong? And if those that would come would not respect your garden, would you not ask them to leave, or build a temporary fence until the garden is strong enough, until it bursts forth with enough fruit so that you can give to even those who do not respect it?

Lesson 1: *The Way That Calls You Home*

Be you therefore, a wise gardener. Cultivate a deep love and respect for yourself, for you are not here to "fix" the world. You are not here to "fix" your brother or sister. It is only love that heals. And until you have loved yourself wholly by having purified the mind of every erroneous thought you have ever held—until you have loved yourself—you do not, in truth, love anyone or anything. Save in those brief moments when you let your guard down and the Love of God shines forth through you so quickly you do not even know what happened! The wise gardener cultivates a state of consciousness in which the Love of God is unimpeded.

Beloved friends, those of you that have elected to answer a call to participate in this pathway, with this family, if you would make your commitment to trusting your Creator for having set before you a pathway that can lead you home, you will, indeed, arrive at home. But commitment means that you do not get to leave the room when the shouting begins. The shouting we are speaking of is the shouting within your own mind, within your own body, within your own emotions.

It means that you will stay with these things by being honest about them, and loving yourself for ever having the power to even create such insane perceptions of yourself and the world around you.

The Way of the Heart is the final pathway that any soul can enter. There are many stages of awakening. There are many pathways that can be followed. But ultimately, "all roads lead to Rome," as they say. Eventually each soul must find its way into The Way of the Heart. Each soul must come back to the truth that it is time to take responsibility; to learn to cultivate the ability to look upon the deep and vicious blackness of what I have called "ego," which is nothing more than the cesspool of denial. It is that which lacks light.

Begin to bring light back to it by simply observing your own mind, your own behavior, and your own reactions with a sense of wonder, with a sense of innocence and with a sense of childlikeness.

For is it not written that you must again become a little child to enter the Kingdom? The little child simply marvels at all that they see and says,

LESSON 1: *The Way That Calls You Home*

"Well, how about that?" Can you imagine looking upon the deepest, darkest parts of your own shadow, your own denials and being able to say, "Oh, how about that!" Remember that everything is neutral, and all that arises within your consciousness has no effect upon the truth of your reality.

The Way of the Heart is a way of cultivating the decision to become identified with the Light that can shine away all darkness. Not by fighting with it, but by recognizing it, embracing it as your own creation, and choosing again. The Way of the Heart is the way that I teach. And now we begin a focused in-depth study together, that this way might become established within your holy mind.

The Way of the Heart Calls You Home

Remember that the Truth is true always. Is it not time, beloved friends, to truly step into ownership of your only reality? The Way of the Heart does not know the word avoidance. It does not know deception, manipulation or control. It does not know blame, although it watches these things arise as echoes of old patterns now outgrown. It learns to see them, to recognize them, like you might recognize certain kinds of clouds that pass through the sky. And then learns to turn the attention of the mind that a new choice might be made.

The Way of the Heart is the way that calls you home. And the call comes from that deep part of your soul that is still like unto the Spirit, which abides as Christ in the holy Mind of God. Trust then, that you are as a sunbeam to the sun. Trust not the perceptions you have cultivated in error. You are not alone on the way that you journey, and you journey not apart from your brothers and sisters. This family cannot know separation. For once the call to awaken through *this* lineage has been acknowledged, though some bodies may not communicate in space and time, rest assured communication remains, and there is no way to avoid it.

We begin, now, The Way of the Heart. It is time to step into the willingness to don the mantle of one committed to healing every obstacle to the presence of Love that may yet remain secretly hidden

Lesson 1: *The Way That Calls You Home*

in the depth of that part of your mind that would struggle to be separate from God. And to remember that you are truly the Light that can come to shine lovingly upon every aspect of darkness you have known.

Along the pathway of this course, you are going to learn how to shake hands with the devil, and to do a little jig with him and recognize his face to be your own. When you can dance with the darkness that you have created, that darkness is transformed into an angel. And light abides with Light.

We will be giving you certain meditations and certain energetic practices to help cultivate within you a quality of feeling that will allow you to recognize energies that do not serve you. These will be given in a way that transcends what your mind may choose to think of these energies, so that you learn more and more to lead with the body, to lead with your feeling nature, not your intellect.

Your intellect does not know anything except the trivialities that you have shoved into it, like garbage into a garbage can. The intellect can never bring the healing of the heart that is the atonement. It can only be utilized to argue against the insane perceptions you are used to, so that you might come to see that perhaps there is a greater good in giving up your insistence on treating the intellect as your god.

Therefore, indeed beloved friends, dance, rejoice and play often. Let these lessons bring up within you everything unworthy of the Mind of Christ—every thought of scarcity, every sense of unworthiness and every fear. Let them come up, look at them, embrace them and transmute them through your own love of Self and through your honesty. Accept where you are and do not pretend to be otherwise. For the wisest are always the humblest.

Be you therefore beloved friends, at peace in all things. For we in what you would call a disembodied state who are electing to participate with those of you who are asking to be helped through this pathway delight in joining with you! We delight in loving you! We delight in waiting on you to welcome your Self home!

I would ask that you close your eyes for just a

Lesson 1: *The Way That Calls You Home*

moment. Take a deep breath into the body and let it go. As the breath leaves the body, hold the thought that there is nothing worth holding onto any longer that keeps your peace and happiness at arm's length. Become committed—fully committed—to the experience of happiness, even as you have been fully committed to unhappiness, limitation and lack. Give your Creator full permission to sweep the basement clean. There really is not anything down there worth defending or protecting.

It will come to pass that you will know the perfect peace of empty-headedness, not-knowingness. You will know what it means to be relieved of time and to be comforted by what is eternal. Never once let yourself think that you are alone. It is nonsense for you to think that I am not with you. You have asked. I have responded. We are in communication. That is the way it is. And that is the way it will be until the end of all illusion.

Peace be unto you always. Amen.

Lesson 2

You Create Your Experience

It is with great joy that I come forth to abide with you. It is a great truth that I come often unto many. But because of what you have learned in your world, you have often believed me to be a figment of your imagination. The voice that steals quietly through the space between your own thoughts, you think to be but an illusion. Yet I say I come often unto many.

I come not alone to commune-i-cate with you. There is, in truth, a host of friends that come to create a vortex, a circumference of energy. We come even as you read these words into your space to set that tone. If you would well receive it, there are many friends unseen by physical eyes that have come forth to contribute and to support this communication.

Why is that important? Always, in each and every moment of your experience, you as a soul, as a divine spark of consciousness, are deliberately choosing to create forms of communication.

What You Perceive Is Communicated Always

You do it with the raiment that you place upon the body. You do it with your gestures and the sound of your voice. You do it with the very culture and time frame in which you incarnate. You are constantly and only creating forms through which you communicate.

Communication is the attempt to rest in communion with creation. What you are choosing to perceive, believe and accept as true will be radiated through you, through your communication devices, which includes the body, that you might transfer your perceptions to another, that they might know who you are and which voice you are committed to.

I have often said that the body is a teaching and learning device, and all forms of communication affect the process of teaching and learning. When you arise in the morning, the first thought that makes a home in your mind, you will act on. You may stretch the body. You may smile. You may frown. You might be filled with peace, or you might feel the weight of the world. These things come, not because you have perceived them *outside*, but because you have allowed them inside the depth of your consciousness that remains pure and undefiled and radiant beyond all boundaries forever.

As that thought makes a home in your mind, you literally begin to transform the communication device called the body into that which carries, expresses and reflects what has come to make a home within your mind. Remember please, that the mind is not where the body is. It does not abide within the body, but the body does abide within the field of your mind.

Communication *is* creation. These two are one and the same. Therefore, if you would create well, ask only:

> What am I committed to communicating?
> What will my creations express?
> What will my creations convey to others?
> For what I seek to convey reveals what I believe is the truth of my Self to the world.

Lesson 2: *You Create Your Experience*

Therefore beloved friends, as we begin to focus on, to refine, to deepen, to mature in The Way of the Heart, it is wise to begin at the beginning. The beginning of this pathway is simply this: You are as God has created you to be. You are an infinite focus of consciousness. Your very sense of existence is nothing more than a feedback loop or feedback mechanism, so that you can witness the effects of the choices you are making in the very deep, deep depth of your mind that rests right alongside the Mind of God.

Therefore, in each moment of your existence, which includes this bodily incarnation, you are literally allowing through deliberate choice—though perhaps unconscious—to bring forth a vibration of thought or a vibration of creation. And to commune-i-cate it to the world in an attempt to experience communion with all of life—with a friend, with a parent, with a child, with a beloved, with the clouds that pass through the sky or with the Earth itself.

Each gesture, each thought, the way that the body breathes, all of these things are going on constantly, and they are communicating or revealing the effect of what you have allowed to make a home in your mind.

Understand well, The Way of the Heart requires that you allow yourself to rest in the simplicity of this truth:

> I am pure Spirit, undefiled and unaffected
> by anything or anyone.
> I am given full power to choose and,
> therefore, to create my experience as
> I would have it be.

Not quite the "I" that is the egoic part of the mind, for that is just one of your creations that came along somewhere down the line. It is a very small part of the mind. We are speaking of the "I" of you that is pure Spirit that knows it exists, even though it does not know the time of its own creation. You are pure Spirit. Therefore to know:

> I am only this, and in each moment,
> regardless of what I believe I see, regard-
> less of the feelings that arise within my
> awareness, I and I alone am wholly one
> hundred percent responsible for them.
> No one has caused them. No great force
> in the universe has made this perception
> well up within my consciousness.
> I have selected it.

Just as you would go to a grocery store and choose what you will have for dinner and then

Lesson 2: *You Create Your Experience*

go home and experience your creation, so too do you choose each experience. When you choose a perception, you lodge it in the mind. Then it expresses itself through the body, through the environment that you create around yourself and through the friends that you would call into your awareness. Every aspect of the life you live is the symbol of what you have chosen to experience and, therefore, to convey throughout creation.

The Way of the Heart begins with the acceptance of this simple truth:

> I am as God created me to be.
> Made in the His image,
> I am a creator always.

What then would you ask your creations to communicate? Why do you make the choices you are making? You all know perfectly well that sometimes you seem to be compelled—and the ego wants you to believe that you are compelled—to certain actions, certain feelings, certain choices, certain perceptions, certain statements by something that surely exists outside yourself. This is *never* true. In *no* circumstance is there anything of creation that has the power to dictate to you the choice you will make.

The Way of the Heart

Peace Flows from Alignment with the Mind of God

Therefore, the pathway of awakening—The Way of the Heart—must start with the decision to embrace the Truth that is true always:

> I am a creator of all that I think and see nd experience.
>
> I am free always. Nothing impinges upon me, but the thoughts I have chosen to hold within.
>
> Nothing imprisons me, but my own perception of imprisonment.
>
> Nothing limits me at any level or dimension of experience, save that which I have chosen.

The Way of the Heart, then, embraces all things, trusts all things and eventually transcends all things. Why? Because it begins by assuming complete and total responsibility for what is being channeled through it. You all serve as a channel, from the moment you arise until the moment you arise. Even during your sleep, you are choosing that which flows through your consciousness.

Lesson 2: *You Create Your Experience*

The goal that we seek has never changed. It is in truth, a journey without distance. It is merely the return to where you are always, that you might begin anew to create deliberately, clearly and with the perfect knowledge that if you are experiencing something, it is because you are the source of it, and for no other reason.

The Way of the Heart is not a way of gaining power. It is not a way in which you will finally be able to make the world be what you want it to be. Rather, it is that pathway in which you learn to transcend and to dissolve from your consciousness every perception, every thought, which is out of alignment with what is true. The thought of death is out of alignment. The thought of fear is out of alignment. The thought of guilt is out of alignment.

The thought of eternal life is *in* alignment. The thought of perfect fearlessness is *in* alignment. The thought of peace is *in* alignment. The realization of innocence is *in* alignment. The thoughts of joy and of forgiveness are *in* alignment and reflect the Truth that is true always.

For although you are given complete free will to create as you choose, the soul begins to learn that what brings it the highest joy, the highest peace, and the highest bliss imaginable is that which flows from the Mind of God through the mind of the channel, the soul, and expresses itself in the field of experience. It is for this reason that the Father's will is that you be happy. And your happiness is found in choosing to restore your perfect alignment with only the voice for God.

The Way of the Heart is that pathway that begins with a commitment to healing and awakening and is founded on the premise, the axiom that we have given unto you:

> You are perfectly free at all times.
> Everything that is experienced has been
> by your choice and at no time has there
> been any other cause.

It seems simple. And yet, what soul has not known resistance to this idea? If you bake a cake and it turns out well, you will say, "I did that." But if you bake a cake and it turns out very bad, you think, "It must have been the flour. It must have been the temperature of the oven. Surely there was something that caused this creation to not be what I would truly desire."

LESSON 2: *You Create Your Experience*

It takes great courage and great faith to look upon all of your creations—your thoughts, your feelings, your manifestations—with love, and with the innocence of a child. For example, to plant a garden and to have all things wither and die, and yet to smile and say, "I planted this garden. I and I alone have done this. Well, I will get a little hungry here, so I might as well go to the store."

Why is this important? Because a long time ago, the soul began to create the perception that it was something other than it was created to be. And the voice for ego emerged within the garden of consciousness. As the soul, that deepest aspect of mind that you have all known, began to identify with a voice that was other than the voice for God, that voice has led you to believe that your creations determine your worthiness. Do you know that feeling?

Therefore, if what you create is not up to snuff, it means that *you*, in the core of your beingness, are some kind of a failure. But I say unto you, in reality, failure is not even remotely possible. Why? If you plant a garden and the seed does not turn into a beautiful flower, but withers and dies, that experience is a creation and you have done it.

And because all events in space and time—everything you experience—are perfectly neutral, there is, in reality, never failure.

The only failure seems to occur within your own consciousness when you believe that it is not acceptable to receive and own and embrace your creation with love and with innocence. Instead you can choose to look upon it, to experience it, and to recognize your perfect safety in doing so. For it is from there, that you can decide whether to continue in that form of creation or whether to think differently and to approach things differently.

That is where the catch is. That part of the mind began to teach you a long, long time ago what to accept as acceptable creations and what to not accept, what to take responsibility for and what to deny responsibility for. And that conflict creates the illusion of separation. When taken to its extreme, one discovers your hospitals full of those in deep depression, paranoia, and the feeling within the being, within the human mind, of feeling alienated and alone.

Helplessness, hopelessness, despair, anger and hatred are all symptoms of a fundamental delu-

Lesson 2: *You Create Your Experience*

sion that has occurred within the depth of the mind. It has occurred because there has been a long history of having cultivated the skill of listening to the wrong voice. The wrong voice is the voice of ego. It has taught you to judge, to pick, to select what you will be responsible for. The more you move into that consciousness, the harder it seems to ever hope for a chance of transcending the sense of separation, conflict and lack of peace.

For how many of you have not known the feeling of resting your head upon the pillow at night and not being able to sleep because it is just not going the way you expected? The reason you cannot sleep is because you are in judgment of your creation.

But it is possible to cultivate just the opposite, in which you learn to look with perfect innocence upon *all* things that arise in the field of your experience. It is possible to look with innocence and wonder at every feeling from the place of curiosity, as you would look upon a cloud that passes through the sky. Look at it, marvel at it—its shape, its color—and embrace it, knowing that it does not affect the purity of the sky through which it temporarily floats.

Each of your creations is exactly like this. It arises in the field of time and space, you experience it, and then it fades away. Every hurt that you have ever known is like a cloud that began to pass into the field of your awareness because you perceived things in a certain way. If that hurt is still lodged within you, it is because you latched on to it. You followed the voice of ego, which caused you to believe that you are identified with that feeling, with that perception. And because you mistakenly thought that was you, you assumed if you let go of it, you might disappear; you might die!

The human mind is that field within creation, within consciousness, that has learned to become so identified with perceptions, experiences and feelings that are not necessarily comfortable, that it believes that if it lets go of them, it will die. From our perspective, as we look upon the energy fields of those of you still identified with this dimension, it looks as though you are gripping, causing energy to condense. Your knuckles are white, trying to hold on to limitation and guilt, to unworthiness and doubt.

You seek innocence and peace. You seek abundance, prosperity and joy. But often, when you

Lesson 2: *You Create Your Experience*

touch these things, it frightens you. Why? Because the Truth of the Kingdom requires openness, trust, expansiveness and spaciousness. It involves allowing, trusting, witnessing and letting things come and go. It involves learning to cultivate a deep enjoyment of whatever arises, seeing that all things are just modifications of consciousness itself, and then letting them go when it is time to do so.

Rest assured, there is no one—not a single soul—who has ever discovered something that was birthed in time that did not also end in time.

How much of your suffering comes because you are clinging to a lifeless past and insisting that you carry it with you still? You are doing that because in the past, you became identified with the clouds that were passing by and claimed that as your own identity. Therefore, if you release it, it will mean that you must change, you must go on.

Creation itself that flows from the Mind of God is ongoing forever! You will never cease to be! You will go on forever and forever and forever and forever and forever. You will go on forever exactly as you are now. Or you can allow the Mind of

God to flow through you, carrying you to an ever-greater expansiveness and deepening your awareness of the infinite loveliness of the power of the Mind of God.

Mastery Arises from Innocence

In these lessons, we will create a system or a pathway upon which you can walk to deliberately cultivate the quality of awareness in consciousness necessary to stabilize that awareness, so that you can bring it to each and every moment of your experience.

Imagine then, being able to experience whatever arises without losing the sense of spaciousness, innocence and ease that you now experience in fleeting moments. For instance, know you the experience when things are going well, you are singing a happy tune, and life seems to be moving ahead? Imagine that same quality of trust, faith, and certainty of purpose, even when the buildings are crumbling around you and the bank account has gone dry. Imagine being able to look at those events with the same sense of innocence and wonder with which you would look into the eyes of your beloved.

LESSON 2: *You Create Your Experience*

For such a quality of awareness is perfect mastery. Within it are discovered perfect peace, perfect freedom, perfect joy and uninterrupted communion with all of creation. And if you would well receive it, that quality of feeling intimately one with all of creation is what you have been seeking as a soul since first the identification with a creation called ego began. For that creation created conflict and separation. Everything you have ever attempted to do since has been an attempt to overcome separation and to gain back what you felt you had lost. It is just that the ways you have sought to do it do not work.

The world of conflict, fear, guilt and unworthiness and the world of the Kingdom lie side by side within your own mind. The eye of the needle that one must pass through is the re-cultivation of the innocence of a child. It is for this reason that I often taught:

> Become again as a little child
> to enter the Kingdom.

The cultivation of The Way of the Heart is that pathway whereby you deliberately and consciously choose to become again as an innocent child. Just as you were in the beginning before you ever created, and then incarnated into, this dimension of experience that seems to be so permeated by a sense of conflict and separation.

What you Decree, Is

I would ask you now to begin to put this into practice. So wherever you happen to be, stop for just a moment and truly become aware of where you are.

Where are you? Are you not having the experience of seemingly being within a body? Do you not seem to be abiding in a room somewhere? Are you not within an environment in which there are certain weather patterns going on around you? Perhaps there are sounds coming into your ears.

Can you truly be aware of where you are now? Can you feel the weight of the body as you stand upon your feet or sit within your chair? Do you notice the tension in the neck? Do you notice the racing of the mind, if that is going on? Can you begin to bring awareness to exactly what *is*, from a place of innocence and non-judgment?

You have a saying in your world, "It is what it

Lesson 2: *You Create Your Experience*

is." That is the beginning of wisdom. You will discover that what *is*, is what you have chosen to make of it. Be, therefore, where you are now, and deliberately decide—deliberately decide—to accept wholly that what you are experiencing in this very moment has no cause whatsoever, except your choice to experience it. Rest assured, whatever the mind may try to say, if you did not wholly want to be right where you are, you would not be there. If you are in a body in the field of space and time, rest assured, you desired it, you chose it, and it is here.

Begin here. There is no need to judge it, no need to ask it to be different. Just truly be aware of what *is*. If you are feeling the body sitting in a chair, allow this thought to come into the mind:

> I have literally created this experience. Something within me is so grand, so powerful, so vast, so beyond anything that scientists have ever come up with, that I have literally crystallized into the field of experience an awareness of being a body in space and time! It has come forth from the field of my consciousness, the gift to me of God, who asks only that I learn to create as God creates.

I have said many times that the Father looks upon you and says:

> This is my only creation and it is very good.

For the Father marvels at what you are, knowing perfectly well that what you are emerged from Her holy mind.

Likewise look upon *your* creations and marvel. How is it that you could abide in this time frame on this planet? How could it be that you can place yourself behind the wheel of an automobile and actually get it from point A to point B? That is a mystery and a marvel, and no one knows how it is done! Yet it is done.

The reason it is done is that all power has been given unto you and what you decree *is*. A man or a woman shall decree a thing and it shall be so. You have decreed this moment. Own it! For by owning it, right now, you can begin to sense the incredible and awesome power that flows through you in each moment. It is the power to create!

Begin by choosing now to cultivate the practice in this manner. Set the intention so that in each hour of your day, for three to five minutes, you practice bringing this quality of awareness to

Lesson 2: *You Create Your Experience*

exactly whatever you are experiencing when the thought arises to do the practice. Where does that thought come from? Imagine you are going through the day and you have been hustling and bustling about. You have gone to your office or your work. You have talked to friends. You have bought groceries. You have done all of these things, and suddenly the thought appears:

> Oh! Focus on being aware that I am literally the creator of what I experience.

Do you think it just happened by accident? No! The thought is penetrating your conscious awareness from the depth of your mind that rests right next to the Mind of God.

Therefore, the power to generate that very thought is the effect of God's will entering into your field of being, penetrating the veils of distraction and shining forth as the thought, "That's right, five minutes every hour." Can you feel the awesomeness of that? For you are linked to the Mind of God, and God knows how to bring you back to complete freedom, perfect peace, and mastery of this entire realm.

Those who truly love God and would truly

awaken will feel something compelling them to master this simple practice for five minutes of each hour. They will learn to delight in and to look forward to it. Pretty soon those five minutes will stretch into six, then ten, fifteen and fifty. Until finally, there is established in their awareness the unchanging realization that everything that arises, they have decreed it, and so it is so.

Five minutes every hour is not much to ask. For five minutes every hour, be as you are created to be—a creator, decreeing that which brings forth experience. Never again allow yourself to say, "Well I'm really here because I have to be. I'm really just doing this because it's what I have to do."

Take the words "ought," "should," "must" and "have to" and write them on a piece of paper. Look at them. Then light a match and light the corner of the paper, and let the paper burn and dissolve to dust. It is a symbol of allowing the energy you have given those words to become again as the dust or the ash of the ground. Clear from your consciousness all identification with such words, for all of them are denials of Reality.

Many times I have shared with you that you *need*

Lesson 2: *You Create Your Experience*

do nothing. Listen to those words, and take them into yourself as though they are your own voice, because they are:

> I need do nothing.

You do not have to survive. Whoever told you that you *had* to? You do not have to make everybody happy. Whoever told you that you had to? Whoever told you that you could make anybody happy? You do not have to abide as a body in space and time. Whoever told you that you had to? You do not have to pay your bills. Who told you that? You literally *need* do nothing.

It is quite different than wanting or choosing to do something. You do not need to love your parents; you do not need to honor your father and your mother. You do not need to worship me or love me. You do not need to love yourself. You literally *need* do nothing, for "need" is an expression of the perception that there is something you lack. Because you are one with God, there is never a moment when you lack anything at all.

Can you allow the thought to emerge in the mind when you arise in the morning: "I *need* do nothing. I don't have to get out of this bed. I don't have to go to an office. I don't need to fulfill that order. I don't need to say, 'Good morning,' to my mate. I literally *need* do nothing."

For how can there be the power of freedom to choose and to create when you are being governed by the belief of the world that you must be a certain way? The belief that you need to be acceptable to others, that you need to conform and fit in, that you need to dress the way others dress, and that you need to be committed to surviving an extra day upon this plane. There can be no freedom where there is need.

Practicing the First Two Axioms

These are the first two axioms of The Way of the Heart, to be built on, to be remembered and to be cultivated daily:

> I am created as my Father created me to be. I am free. And nothing sources my experience but me in each moment. Nothing has an effect upon me whatsoever, save that which I choose to allow to affect me.
>
> I need do nothing.

Lesson 2: *You Create Your Experience*

In the beginning we would suggest that you practice this second axiom in the morning and in the evening, as you are arising and as you are retiring. At least twice in each of your days, we ask you to cultivate for five minutes the repetition of this thought so that you feel it in your bones: I need do nothing.

It will come as quite a shock to your consciousness. The mind will say, "But I have all these things I have to do! What about this and what about that? Oh, my goodness! Will the world stop spinning if I stop needing?" That is up to the world, not up to you.

The power of these first two axioms will be what everything that follows is built on. Yet everything that follows is merely a way of watering those two axioms and making them the anchor of your awareness.

For when the anchor is firmly in place, you will literally create whatever you so desire from perfect freedom and from perfect deliberateness. You will even transcend miracle mindedness. For miracle mindedness is still a stage of perception just short of mastery. Mastery comes when you know that you are literally and deliberately creating. There is nothing miraculous about it. You will decree a thing and it shall be so!

That is to create as God creates. For while He marvels at you, He knows perfectly well that your creation was not a miracle. It was very deliberate, born from the pure radiance of Love. God does not sit on His throne and say, "I wonder if I am worthy to create my children? I wonder if I am worthy to express myself through the divine spark of consciousness that they are?"

Never does it enter into the holy Mind of God, "I wonder if it is okay if I create a solar system?" God receives a thought or a thought emanates within His holy Mind, He decrees it, and it is so! And He looks upon all things and says, "It is very good!"

Exercise in Conscious Creation

The third and last exercise that we would give you in this lesson is this: Choose something that you do every day, that you are convinced is so utterly ordinary that it certainly does not hold any power or any spiritual meaning whatsoever.

LESSON 2: *You Create Your Experience*

It could be something as simple as having a glass of water, brushing your teeth or yawning.

Pick something that you know you do every day and decide to make that the focus of your worship. So that when you do it, you stop and say, "It is very good." Even if it is something as simple as raising your head from the pillow. Become aware of it, own it as self-created, and as you contemplate that action, say to yourself, "It is very good. I have done this, and it is good. I have created."

Again, those that are truly committed will find that they begin to enjoy this process, and they begin to apply it more and more to other events in their lives. They begin to reawaken the childlike joy of building a castle in the sandbox. For in truth, that is all you are doing here. Consciousness is your sandbox and you are creating castles. You have simply forgotten to enjoy them.

When you want to be rid of them, you now lament, "Oh, but if I give this up and change my mind and move on, what will happen to my creations? What will others think of me if I act like a child and just take my little plastic shovel and knock the castle down and go in and have a sandwich for lunch? What will people think of me? Will I fit in? Will I be accepted? Will I be judged? Will I be persecuted?" Who cares! For the opinions of others mean nothing, unless of course, you want them to mean something.

Now we come to what concludes this lesson. What blocks you in your mind? For even as you are reading this, you may recognize a resistance. That resistance is the energy of fear: "What will happen if I follow this path?" That part of your mind called the ego will rise up to tell you that if you listen to the one that some have called the savior of the world, it will take you to a path of destruction. That is because the voice of ego knows that it will be destroyed if this path is followed. You—the reality of who you are—cannot be destroyed.

That resistance is fear. And fear is one of the energies out of alignment with the truth of the Kingdom. Therefore, fear not, but continue in faith. For I say unto you, what you will discover at the end of this pathway is perfect freedom, perfect power, perfect spaciousness, perfect joy and perfect peace of living—literally—in the Kingdom of Heaven.

The choice is yours. For those of you that will feel

Lesson 2: *You Create Your Experience*

this resistance come up so strongly and for those of you that will yet call out unto me in your dreams and your prayers, "Help me through this," I say unto you that you walk not alone. For I cannot be further from you than the width of a thought. And yes, you are the creator of that thought.

I, too, embarked upon just such a path. Each axiom that I will share and refine as well as many of the exercises in *The Way of Mastery* are specifically exercises and truths that were given to me from the time I was initiated by certain Essene teachers in The Way of the Heart.

When my teachers said, "It is time for you to go spend forty days and forty nights in the desert," do you not believe that resistance came up within me too? I, too, had to notice that I was creating a thought of fear and separating myself from the great protection and Love of God. I had to physically move the body into the wilderness to move through my own rings of fear to discover what was on the other side.

The pathway that I have walked is the pathway that you are walking. And if our pathway is the same, then we walk together to God and away from illusion, pain, weakness, unworthiness, guilt and death.

So engage in your exercises with great zeal, with great joy and above all, with great outrageous playfulness! Learn to look with innocence upon all that arises. Abide lovingly with your creations. If you put these little exercises to work, much indeed, *will* arise. Practice, then, well. And practice with joy.

Know that you are loved, loving and lovable, and that, in truth, the only thing that is occurring is that an old dream is being released that a new dream might replace it—the dream of worthiness, peace, wakefulness and union with all of creation.

Again, I say, I come not alone in this specific work, but I come with many who support your healing and your awakening.

Therefore indeed be at peace this day, beloved friends. Abide *lovingly* with your creations. Amen.

Lesson 3

The Power of Forgiveness

If I search the languages of your world, I cannot find the words that can convey the Love that I feel for you. I cannot find the words that can convey unto you the Love that God has for all of us. I cannot find a concept, a word, an idea, a philosophy or a dogma that can contain the mystery that is closer to you than your own breath and awaits your discovery.

If I search throughout all of creation, if I search through the many mansions that exist within the domains of my Father's creation—and that creation is infinite—try as I might, I cannot discover anything that can truly describe *you*. I cannot find anything that is of greater value than you. In truth, I cannot discover anything that speaks more eloquently of the Love that God is than your very existence. Therefore, in truth, I look upon you constantly, and marvel at the radiance of my Father's Love. It is through *you* that I come to discover all that God is.

When I walked upon your Earth as a man, I began to realize that the greatest gift that I could ever receive would only come to me as I chose to surrender every perception that I might conjure up about you, my brother or sister, that would *veil* the Truth that is true about you always.

When I was nine years of age, I began to awaken to exactly what I am describing to you. As my father would take me to sit with the elders and as he would read from the Torah to me, I began to be compelled by something within. Something began to speak to me, that underneath all of the perceptions that I could create of another, there was something radiant and shimmering waiting to be discovered.

I began to feel very different from my peers. I began to be preoccupied with inner things. When I listened to the elders speak, I would often feel as though I had drifted far away from where they were. Pictures would come to me, thoughts would come to me, and feelings would come to

Lesson 3: *The Power of Forgiveness*

me that I did not understand, that I had not assimilated into my being.

But something began to compel me. How might I discover how to see *only* that shimmering radiance? Would it be possible for me to see my brothers and sisters as my Father sees His children? I discovered that the way to see with the eyes of Christ begins with the acceptance that I, as a creator—created in the image of God—literally choose every experience and call it to me, that I create the veils through which I view creation.

I began to shift my perspective slightly. And I began to be seen as someone who was rebelling against the teachings of my Essene elders. For I began to move away from *striving* for God, *striving* for perfection, and began to cultivate within myself the process of <u>*allowing*</u>.

I discovered that if I looked upon my perceptions, my feelings, my behavior exactly as they were without overshadowing them with my own interpretations—if I could teach myself to embrace things with innocence—veils began to be dissolved from my mind.

For when I was nine years old, I had already learned to be fearful of thinking, speaking or acting in a way that was not in conformity to the prevailing wisdom of that time—even within the Essene community, which had become rather rigidified. There was already much dogma. And dogma always leads to bickering.

I began to discover that if I looked with innocence upon all things, a light began to shine *through* the things I was looking at. And as I rested more and more in this innocence, more and more the light would shine.

As I grew in age, I discovered that the old teachers who spoke of the need to "forgive seventy times seven" knew something quite profound that had even become lost within the Jewish and Essene traditions of my day.

For to forgive means to choose to release another from the perceptions you have been projecting upon them. It is, therefore, an act of forgiving *one's self* of one's projections. As you begin to forgive—even seventy-times-seven times—each time you forgive, you take yourself deeper into the purity of your own consciousness. You begin

Lesson 3: *The Power of Forgiveness*

to see how profoundly you have been coloring and, therefore, affecting all of your relationships, through the simple act of not being aware of the power of projection.

Therefore, I learned—and learned well—that forgiveness is an essential key to healing. The opposite of forgiveness is judgment, and judgment always creates separation and guilt. Judgment will evoke a sense of guilt in the one that has been judged, unless they are perfectly awake.

But more than this, each time that you judge anything or anyone, you have literally elicited guilt within *yourself*. Because there is a place within you, yet still, that knows the perfect purity of your brother and sister, and sees quite clearly that all things within the human realm are either the extension of love or a cry for help and healing.

When you judge, you have moved out of alignment with what is true. You have decreed that the innocent are not innocent. And if you would judge another as being without innocence, you have already declared that this is true about you! Therefore, to practice forgiveness actually cultivates the quality of consciousness in which you finally come to forgive yourself. And it is indeed the forgiven who remember their God.

We wish to share with you the power of forgiveness: How to cultivate it, how to refine it, how to understand the depths of it that can be revealed to you as you forgive seventy-times-seven times and how to bring up within you that which has not yet been forgiven, but perhaps forgotten. In this lesson, we will also speak of what perception is and what projection is.

Beloved friends, these things are of critical importance. For anyone who enters into a so-called "spiritual path" must eventually face and deal with their deep need for forgiveness, which is an expression of the soul's deep desire to be forgiven. For there is no one who walks this Earth who has not been touched by the poison of judgment.

As we speak of these things, let not seriousness enter the mind. For in truth, all we are really doing is describing what you need to do—and can do—to release the burden of illusion that seems to cause you to feel a heaviness upon your countenance and a sense of a lack of safety in the world. You could think of it as taking your rheostat and

Lesson 3: *The Power of Forgiveness*

turning it up a bit by *enlightening* you—taking your burden of guilt and judgment from you.

Therefore, in truth, understand well. Forgiveness is essential. What has not been forgiven in others, has not been forgiven in you. But not by a God who sits outside of you, for He never judges. What you have not forgiven in another or in the world is but a reflection of what you carry within as a burden that you cannot forgive of *yourself*.

You have an interesting saying in your world: "It takes one to know one." Do you think you would even be able to judge another if there was not something within you being elicited that triggers within you the belief that you know exactly what that other one is up to? That is why you judge them. Sometimes you judge harshly because you fear that energy in yourself. Or you remember how hurtful you have been when you have acted from that energy.

But when you have forgiven yourself, rest assured, you will know what it means to walk in this world yet not be *of* this world. You will be able to feel the energy or the activities that any other soul may freely choose. You will discern that energy, you will understand that energy, and you will see through it and still see the face of Christ before you.

You will not react, which literally means to act again, as you did in the past. Instead, even if you are being persecuted (or to speak from personal experience, to be nailed upon a cross), you will have cultivated the ability to love. And in all situations, no matter what another is doing, your first response will be to enter into the quiet stillness within and merely ask the Holy Spirit:

> What would you have me say?
> What is most appropriate for this other
> soul in this moment?

For when forgiveness has purified the mind and the heart and the emotional field of your own being, you will discover that you exist only to extend Love.

You are the savior of the world. In each situation, your role is to ask the Holy Spirit how you can serve the atonement, the correction, the healing that yet needs to be acquired within another soul. So even if one hates you, you will not respond with defensiveness, but with curiosity, with innocent witnessing. Even if your hands have nails going through them, I tell you truthfully that it is possible to still enter the quiet sanctuary of the heart and to ask of the Holy Spirit:

> What would you have me say or
> do that can serve the healing of
> my brother or sister's heart?

All that I will be sharing with you, not just in this lesson, but in this course, has as its final goal your complete Christed consciousness and the fulfillment of what your own soul desires—forgiveness.

Forgiveness, the Bridge to the Soul of Your Brother and Sister

There is nothing you can be aware of in the energy of another that you have not known in yourself. There is nothing another can say or do, or even imagine themselves capable of saying or doing that you have not also known. Again, it takes one to know one. When you perceive another acting out of hostility or fear, the only way you can recognize it is because you have been there.

The very fact that in your world one can murder

another's body and you can react with knowledge that that is inappropriate behavior is because as a soul, you know the energies involved in the attempt to murder another. If you are honest with yourself, you can probably come up with at least fifty times in the last year that murderous thoughts have entered your mind. You may not act on them. You may not even dwell on them for more than a split second, but the energy has come into the field of your awareness, and you have known it and recognized it.

Who then is less than you? Who then is worthy of your judgment? No one. Who then is equal to you? Everyone. And who then is worthy of your love? Everyone.

Forgiveness is the bridge that links you to the soul—the essence—of your brother or sister. Forgiveness is that bridge that when cultivated will allow you to see clearly. Not just the energies that another is expressing, but you will literally be able to see what events seemed to cultivate that soul's belief that they must act in that way to survive, and what perceptions have led them to feel justified in their inappropriate behaviors.

LESSON 3: *The Power of Forgiveness*

You will see it as clearly as though someone had drawn a picture in front of you.

Then you will see skillfully what to say and what to do to gently help another correct their misperceptions of themselves and learn the path of self-forgiveness. And when that hour comes, rest assured you will walk in this world, yet you will not be in it. You will be as I became. You will be the savior of the world.

The Veil of Projection

What is projection? Projection occurs when there has first been denial within yourself. Projection is an act in which you psychically try to throw out of your ownership everything that you have judged as being despicable or unworthy of you—something you do not want. So you will project it. You will throw it up and out and let it land on whomever happens to be nearby. Projection is the effect of the denial of the first axiom that I have given you. It is the denial of the truth that:

> Nothing you experience has been caused
> by anything outside of you.

Projection is the attempt to insist that reality is other than the way God made it. That you are not powerful, that you are a victim of circumstances, that you are in a world that can actually do things to you and cause you to make decisions that you would not have made otherwise. That is always denial. And it is a lie.

Again, projection is the denial of the first axiom of truth, and you have mastered it well. When you project onto another, you will then believe that your anger or your hatred is justified.

In fact, the legal system means merely to take the act of projection and the need to judge and to make it okay socially, so that you need not be concerned with this other as your brother or as your sister who has been crying out for help. Rather, you become justified in punishment. Yet punishment is only the insane attempt to convince the punisher that the darkness, the evil—whatever you want to call it—is not in them, it is *out there*.

Imagine then, a society in which the prevalent legal view is simply that your brother or your sister is an aspect of yourself. And if you would help yourself, you must help them—meeting each cry

Lesson 3: *The Power of Forgiveness*

for help and healing with forgiveness, love and support. Can you imagine, for a moment, what it would be like to live in such a society? How would it be different than the world you see?

If you would have these things be different, it must begin with you. For the way to heal the world is not by seeking to change what is on the outside, but by first changing what is on the inside. When *that* change has occurred, you will become a conduit for an energy that knows how to use your gifts, and how to place you in just the right situations. And a great power will work effectively through you—the power alone that knows how to heal your world.

There are many that would love to march for peace by angrily attacking those who make war. But if you would create peace in the world, you must be at peace within yourself.

Projection is an act of trying to get rid of what you do not want to own within. It is the effect of the denial of truth. Projection colors your brother or sister with the very energies that you would judge within yourself. How can you begin to break the pattern of projection? How can you allow the bridge of forgiveness to be built? It is actually quite simple, but it will require your commitment.

Awakening Requires Vigilance and Discipline

I have said to you many times that the world you see is nothing more than the effect of the thoughts you have held within the mind. Therefore, awakening requires the act of vigilance and discipline. The discipline to cultivate a way of living in which you observe your own thoughts, in which you listen to the words that are coming out of your mouth, in which you observe the feelings that are evoked within your body, the reactivity that seems to own you, and to see these things as innocent and simply self-caused.

When next something is reflected to you by the world that causes you to become angry or causes you to be in judgment, stop right where you are and look, not with judgment of your judgment, but with innocence and honesty:

> Oh, I see that I am judging someone. That is an interesting cloud passing through the

LESSON 3: *The Power of Forgiveness*

> sky of my awareness. I wonder if I might
> be able to make another choice.

Now the mind will tell you, "But this person just broke into my house and stole my stereo. Of course, I have a right to be in judgment! I have a right to feel angry."

But I say unto you, anger is never justified. It does not mean you will not experience it. But stop fooling yourself into believing that there is some validity to it. When someone has just broken into your home and taken your stereo equipment (or some other idol that you love), what if you understood that you had the power in that moment to remember that all events are neutral? They merely provide you with a chance to choose Love.

What if you literally chose the "insane" way, according to the world, of looking upon that one who has just done that act as a brother or sister who is crying out for help and healing? What if you chose to look upon them as one who does not know how to live *in* this world without being *of* the world, who does not know the way to self-forgiveness, who does not know the truth of the

Light that lives within them, and who does not recognize their great power to create whatever they want in a way that is not hurtful to anyone? What if you chose to look upon them with compassion rather than reactivity?

It begins in simple ways. To set the stage, I want you to remember that time has been given to you that you might use it constructively. That means when you awaken in the morning, realize that you are in school. You do not have to drive anywhere; you are already there!

The universe is literally helping to assist you into having experiences that will bring things up for you so that you can choose to look at them differently; thereby, discovering the great power within you—the freedom within you to choose what you want to perceive and to elicit only what you want to feel. So that even if nails are being driven through the hands, you finally are liberated in the power to choose Love, and therefore, to overcome this world.

Having said this, understand that each of your days is a blessing and a gift, if you use it from the full commitment to awakening. Your day is

Lesson 3: *The Power of Forgiveness*

chock full of a million opportunities to discover a deeper truth. Therefore, never feel that the purpose of your life must be something other than what you are involved in. For remember what we spoke of earlier:

> You are literally creating everything you choose and nothing is forced upon you.

Now we are going to take that thought just a little deeper for a moment. It literally means that if you have decided you want to awaken, you have already called to yourself every experience that can truly best serve your awakening. The friends, family and people you have relationships with are those who likewise can best gain from the experiences elicited through relationship with you. It means that right here and right now you are already demonstrating the power that you are seeking—the power to truly choose to awaken, and to command the whole of creation to serve you in that awakening.

Therefore, when you awaken in each of your mornings, look around. Who is that person sleeping next to you? They are your perfect companion. They are a messenger of God. For just behind your experiences, there is something deeper taking place. Because your mind is resting right next to the Mind of God, when you first said as a soul, "I want to awaken, I want to go home," the Father answered your prayer and began to send the thought through your Spirit and through your soul to your conscious mind:

> I know how to direct you home.
> Give up this career and start that one.
> Move from this location to that location.

You began to feel all manner of impulses. You began to read different books. You began to do different things. You met someone and fell in love. All by accident? Hardly!

The very thought that you would claim as your own from which you have created the world of your own personal experience is also literally the result of your prayer to awaken. And the Father is creating—assisting you to create—just those experiences as stepping stones that carry you from where you are to where God is.

The result is that your ordinary daily life is the most perfect ashram you could ever be within. It

Lesson 3: *The Power of Forgiveness*

is the holy city to which it is wise to make pilgrimage every day, which means to bring awareness and commitment to exactly what you are experiencing. To be thankful for it, to bless it, to embrace it, to be vigilant and to be mindful:

What is this moment teaching me?

Having given that as background and foundation, remember that you do not experience anything that is called an "ordinary moment." In each and every moment, extraordinary things are occurring. Extraordinary things are occurring in which the whole of the universe is conspiring, which means to "breathe together." The universe is conspiring with you to awaken you and to heal you. Trust it! Love it!

That these things are true—and I assure you that they are—means that your life, the very life you are living is equal in power and majesty and effectiveness to any life that has ever been lived. It means that your very life is equal to the one that I lived. For it is bringing you home, as my life was my pathway home to God.

To build on what I shared earlier, the third axiom

or principle could be encapsulated in this way:

> I do not live any ordinary moments.
> With each breath, my experiences are
> the stepping stones laid before me of
> God to guide me home.
> I will bring awareness to each moment
> and allow it to teach me how to forgive,
> how to embrace, how to love and therefore how to live fully.

In your ordinary moments, a thousand times each day, you will be confronted by opportunities to be disturbed! And in that very same moment, you are being given the blessing of the opportunity to choose peace, to remember to cultivate a perception of your brother or sister that is a perception birthed out of the Christ Mind, not the egoic mind.

Forgiveness, then, can be practiced diligently. And you will not need to look too far. You will not need to make a pilgrimage to some far city. You do not need to go sit in a cave in the mountains somewhere to discover the way to God. It is all around you, because you can only be where you have decreed to be. You have decreed to be there because you, as a soul, truly want nothing

LESSON 3: *The Power of Forgiveness*

more than to awaken. Your life, just as it is unfolding moment-to-moment, is meant for *you*.

If this is true, and I assure you that it is, the way to God can only be found in your willingness to embrace and live *fully* the very life that is within you and that unfolds through you with each moment. To live without fear, to go forward, to indeed trust and embrace the very power and the majesty that is the seed, the soil and the ground from which your life's experience is unfolding. It is precious! It is extraordinary! It is blessed! And it is given to you of God!

Would you not embrace the blessing of your life and sanctify it to keep it holy and recognize that your life is worthy of your respect? It does not matter what anybody else thinks. It matters what *you* think.

Beloved friends, your life—your life—is your way home! If you do not live it fully, how can you ever arrive home? Therefore, fear not your greatness. Fear not the power that comes from embracing your life and claiming its value. Live it full out with every bit of passion you can muster! Embrace every second of it! Every time you wash your dish and your cup after breakfast, look upon these things and say:

> My God! This is my life!
> This is my pathway home!
> And I am going to live it!

Precious friends, in this way you will come to forgive yourself of the judgments you have made. For who among you has not known the feeling of saying, "God, my life is just not worth very much. I will never be like so-and-so down the street. I will never have enough money. Not enough people are going to know me. When will *my* work ever get out as big as *that* person's work?" And on and on!

But I say unto you, every time you have judged yourself, you have weakened yourself. Every time you have judged yourself or another, you have slipped down the mountain another notch, when your desire is to be at the summit.

How Forgiveness Heals

Understanding these things, let us look more closely at forgiveness. How does it work? What really occurs when you forgive?

LESSON 3: *The Power of Forgiveness*

You are a conduit of energy. To the degree that the conduit is in perfect working order, the energy can flow so radiantly that the conduit actually becomes transparent. That is, it no longer blocks. There is no barrier or limit to the Light.

When you judge, it is as though you contracted and made the walls of the conduit smaller, just like building up rust in your pipes. And the flow becomes less and less.

As you forgive judgments, it is as though the rust in the pipes is dissolving. It is as though the walls of the pipe that are carrying the liquid of God's Love begin to expand and become thinner and thinner and more transparent.

Judgment is contraction.

Forgiveness is relaxation, peace, trust and faith.

Forgiveness allows the spaciousness within your consciousness to grow. For when you look upon the thief that has broken into your home and say, "I forgive you," you are decreeing the *opposite* of what you have learned. You are decreeing that nothing can be taken from you of any value. You are decreeing that judgment is the opposite of what you want, and it will cause you to feel the opposite of how you want to feel. You are decreeing your power to perceive differently. You are, therefore, healing yourself.

If you ever want to come home, you are going to have to become very, very divinely selfish. You are going to have to become so selfish that you will not tolerate judgment in yourself—of anyone or anything. Because you will begin to recognize that every such act catapults you to the other side of the universe from where you want to be.

Judgment causes the very cellular structure to break down. If you could see this, you would never judge again. When you judge, even the cells of your body go crazy. They vibrate in a completely dissonant way. There is contraction. The fluids do not move through the cells. The nutrients do not become transported or delivered to the cells. The waste matter is not processed properly. Everything gets clogged up, and there is dis-ease.

Therefore, beloved friends, understand well that judgment is not something to take lightly. Should you, then, judge yourself if you have noticed you

Lesson 3: *The Power of Forgiveness*

have been in judgment? No. That is a judgment in itself. Only Love can heal. Therefore, when you know you have judged, simply say:

> Ah, yes! That is that energy.
> I recognize that cloud that has just passed
> through the field of my awareness.
> But I can choose again.

So how does this work? If in your "ordinary" daily life—that we now know is not ordinary at all—you detect that you have been in judgment of someone or something, recognize that that judgment is still with you. It is a present thing, even though you may have enacted it five minutes ago, or fifty-five years ago or ten lifetimes ago. When you notice it or bring awareness to it, you have made it a very present thing. So it is right there in front of you to be undone. And that is what you need to focus on:

> I am going to choose again.

You know the experience of looking back in your life, and suddenly seeing a scene in which *now* you know you behaved selfishly from ego, and that you were manipulative or cunning or hurtful? Or you recognize, "My God, I was really in judgment of that person. Oh, if only I could go back and undo it." Know you that feeling?

I say unto you, you *can,* because everything is present. There is no such thing as past and future, there is only *now*. So when you have that thought or that memory, it is coming to you for a very specific reason. As a soul, you are learning about forgiveness and how to undo the effects of your previous choices. And so it is being presented to you, yet again, that you might make a new choice.

When that old memory comes, stay with it. Look at it. Recognize how judgment worked at that time. And then say to that person or that event:

> I judge you not.
> I extend forgiveness to myself
> for what I have created.
> I embrace you, and I love you.
> I free you to be yourself.
> I bless you with the blessing of Christ.

Then see that image or that memory begin to gently dissolve into light, until there is no trace of it left. And be done with it.

LESSON 3: *The Power of Forgiveness*

Right away the mind says, "But when I kicked that little boy in the shins when I was four years old just to watch him scream…he is not here." Isn't he? The *body* is not here, but the body is not quite the soul.

All minds are joined. It means that where you extend forgiveness within the consciousness, within your emotional field to another—whether they be physically present or not—you *are* extending to them exactly what you could extend to them if they were physically in front of you.

Even if they were, they still have to receive it, do they not? They still have *their* choice to make—whether to accept your forgiveness or to remain in judgment of *you*. And that is their issue, not yours.

Understand then, that you are dealing with consciousness. You are not a physical being, you are Spirit. And you are intimately linked with all minds and all times. Therefore, forgiveness of another can occur anytime that you decide it can occur. Anyone you have ever believed has wronged you can be forgiven by you in this very moment. Anytime you have judged another and, therefore, been in judgment of yourself, you can undo that in the very present moment, simply by making a different choice.

Reactivity Indicates the Need for Self Forgiveness

Rest assured, you will continue to project upon others what remains unhealed and unforgiven within yourself. Each time you react to another, you are being given a sign that there is some kind of energy that has been presented to your awareness that you have not forgiven within yourself. If someone is critical and you react every time they are critical, rest assured, you have not healed that part of your own being—that part of your own experience of being critical of others.

Whether it is occurring now, or whether it seems to be a pattern that you have interrupted and no longer do, you have still not forgiven yourself for having identified with that energy.

Use your ordinary experience in each day to observe what pushes your buttons. We will give you a very simple technique for doing so. If you will stay with it, it will reveal to you the energies that are in need of your forgiveness.

LESSON 3: *The Power of Forgiveness*

The technique is quite simple. As you go through your day, observe when you feel as though you are in contraction. Are the muscles of the body tight? Is the breath very shallow? Does your voice become faster or louder when you speak about some energy in someone else? That is a sign that you need to do healing within yourself. When you recognize that these kinds of signs are going on—in other words, life has presented you with an opportunity to be disturbed—that is a sign that there is something that requires healing. Therefore, count it a blessing if you feel disturbed.

Healing Exercise

Turn your awareness from what you think is causing the disturbance and remember the first axiom:

> I am the source of my experience.
> I am feeling disturbed.
> What is it in me that needs to be healed?

Begin to breathe deeply and rhythmically. Let the body soften and relax, and ask:

> What is it within this person's energy that is really causing my reaction?

You will see it right away: "Oh, they are so critical. Criticism pushes my buttons."

Then ask yourself:

> When have I done that to another?
> Where have I been critical of others?

And it might hit you right away: "Well, I'm being critical because they're critical."

Or memories will come back, distasteful memories, if you are judging them. Let them come back. Continue to breathe and relax. Look upon that energy of being critical. Honor it. Love it. For it is a creation. It is your creations coming back to you, that you might embrace them and transform them. Just stay with it. Look at it: "Ah, being critical, yes, I can sure be critical. I've been that way in the past. I know that energy very well."

Look upon a scene in your memory in which *you* have been the one being critical. Look upon it with deep honesty and sincerity, and say to yourself:

> I forgive me for being critical.
> I forgive my judgment of myself.
> I choose to teach only Love.

LESSON 3: *The Power of Forgiveness*

Watch that image dissolve and disappear from your mind. Bring your awareness back to the present moment and that person that just pushed your button. Again, you do not need to say anything to them at all, although you might. But within yourself, forgive them for allowing the energy of being critical to temporarily make a home in their mind. And merely ask the Holy Spirit to replace your perception with the truth. Ask to see the innocent light within them.

As you cultivate this, you will become very, very good at it. You will be able to do it as fast as the time it takes to snap your fingers. And once you begin to see the light in them, you can ask the Holy Spirit:

What is this critical energy in them masking?
What are they really crying out for?

Then you will feel compassion. For it will be revealed to you why they are hurting inside. And low and behold, instead of being reactionary toward them, you just might be compassionate. Your choice of words and your own behavior might turn out to be different than you could have ever imagined. For through you will flow exactly what serves them.

The Way of the Heart

When I was being nailed to the cross, there was one who raised the mallet to strike the nail. And as he raised the mallet, his eyes met mine for just a moment. I did exactly what I have described to you. By this time I had mastered this so it was done very quickly. I asked myself, "How have *I* ever wanted to drive a nail through someone else?" And I remembered my murderous thoughts. I forgave myself and brought my attention back to that one, and asked only to see the light in him. And I asked:

What is it that this action is mirroring to me?
What is it masking within him?

And I saw that one's soul, and I loved that one's soul. And I felt compassion for that one. In that moment—mark my words—in that moment of eye contact, that one got it!

Because my energy was different, it created the space in which that soul could make a new choice. That soul saw suddenly the entirety of its experience, and realized that if it allowed that mallet to fall upon the nail, it would be a decision to choose to continue being nothing more than a doormat for other people's perceptions. And in

LESSON 3: *The Power of Forgiveness*

that very instant, that soul decided to follow a path that would lead to sovereign mastery, and never again be a pawn of any government, or any group, or any faction or anyone. He dropped the mallet from his hand—this was a Roman soldier—stood up, walked away and disappeared.

That one has gone on to become a master that is known by literally thousands of beings. He is not in physical form. This one visits many, teaches many. This one indeed incarnated perfect mastery and, therefore, transcended the world. And it all began as the result of *my* desire to teach only Love. Now, we have a very good friendship.

So you see, you may not know how powerful your choice for healing is. You may not really see how deeply and profoundly it will affect you, as you go on being a creator—and you go on forever. You could never possibly know what fruits will be born from that tree in the life of another. But because all minds are joined, when *you* choose healing through forgiveness, you literally create the space in which the *other* can also heal their life.

Let no moment then be wasted. See nothing as ordinary. And see not the perceptions taught to you of the world being justified within yourself. But be wholly committed to rooting up and out of your being anything that is unlike the Love of Christ. Think not that I am the only one that can love this way—it is not true. You are here to love as I learned to love. Why? Because you *are* that Love. Everything else is just a smoke screen.

Forgiveness is necessary. Forgiveness is a skill and an art that will pay you dividend upon dividend upon dividend upon dividend. It will never cease in paying you. Each moment in which you choose forgiveness, you have literally saved yourself a thousand years of suffering! I mean that about as literally as one can mean it. In short, every act of forgiveness is a miracle that shortens the need for experience in this dimension.

When you find yourself in a situation that you believe is too big, rest assured, it is because something big has finally come to the surface to be healed within you so that more power can shine forth through you. Why? You have reached the place where you are ready for it. More of Christ can be lived.

LESSON 3: *The Power of Forgiveness*

Ending Your Day

It is very, very important to let each day be sufficient unto itself. When you end your day, always truly end it. Do not take four hours of ritual. You can do it within one breath. As you take a deep breath as you rest your head upon the pillow, look upon the whole day, embrace it with your consciousness, and as you let your breath go out, say silently to yourself:

> I release and forgive this day. It has been perfect. And it is done.

Let it go. Just let it go. Why? If you do not, you will just bring it with you. Know you that experience? And for three weeks, you are lamenting, "Oh gosh, why did I make that decision three weeks ago? If I had only made a different decision, this would not have happened and that would not have happened." That is probably true. But the point is now three weeks later, you are still hitting yourself over the head by bringing the past with you. And you miss the glory of the present. You have all heard that a thousand times because it is the truth.

Consciousness is a very subtle and powerful thing. You cannot help but create. Remember the goal of this pathway is to learn to deliberately create with perfect mastery. Therefore, look upon the things of the day and say:

> It is very good. And it is finished.

Each night when you rest your head upon the pillow and you know you are about to go off to sleep, be just like God in your Biblical story of creation, in which it is written that on the seventh day, God rested. God was finished, in a sense, within the story. Have that same quality at the end of each of your days.

If you are carrying some kind of emotional reaction because of something someone said or did, or something you said or did, practice forgiveness before you sleep. If you do not, you will keep experiencing the conflicted energies during your dream states. And communication between you and the other one, who has not yet been forgiven, will keep going on until that forgiveness is complete within you.

LESSON 3: *The Power of Forgiveness*

It is *very* important. Time should never be taken frivolously. Play with it, yes, but play with it out of consciousness, out of clarity, out of recognizing that there is no such thing as an idle thought. Each thought creates a world of experience for you. And you are worthy of experiencing Heaven.

We will have much more to say about forgiveness as we begin to plumb the depths of what is discovered as you practice forgiveness seventy-times-seven times. It takes you deeper and deeper into the very mechanics of consciousness itself—the very mechanics of creation. Put forgiveness at the top of your list until you know how perfectly forgiven you are. Be, therefore, vigilant against denying what is still in need of forgiveness within you. For what you deny, you will project. And each projection is a hurtful act to *yourself*. Of course, it is also hurtful to the other, but primarily to yourself.

There is much that has been said in this lesson that needs to be read again and again so that the mind begins to truly grasp how important and how powerful forgiveness is. You will reach a place where you absolutely delight in going through your day expressing forgiveness, like a wave emitting itself from the ocean of your consciousness, even if nobody is doing anything. Forgiveness, itself, becomes a delightful energy to live within.

Beloved friends, forgive *yourself* well and you have forgiven Christ. When Christ is forgiven, Christ will arise and make His home in your heart, your mind and even in the cells of your body. You will know what it means to walk *in* this world yet not be of the world. And when you look in the mirror, you will say:

> Behold, the savior appears.

It will not be egoic arrogance that says it, but the recognition of what is true always:

> I am my Father's child and I am sent into this world to bring light to it.

Be you, therefore, at peace. Practice forgiveness well, until it becomes like taking a breath. You will discover power that you did not know could exist, and a freedom whose taste is sweet above

Lesson 3: *The Power of Forgiveness*

honey. I forgive you. Not because I have judged you, but because I know the blessing that forgiveness brings to me. Forgiveness is something I perfected as a man. Perfect it within yourself as well, and you will know the glory of Christ.

Be you therefore at peace, beloved friend. Amen.

LESSON 4

FOLLOWING THE THREAD OF DESIRE

It is with great joy that I walk with you on the way that you have chosen. For in truth, there is not a time that I am not with you. There is not a place to which you can journey where you will not discover my presence.

Only reality can be true. And reality is simple: there is but the simplicity of Love. From that ocean there is birthed a multitude of forms, a multitude of worlds, a multitude of creations, of which you are one. Like waves arising from the sea, those creations remain linked eternally to their Creator.

You are a wave arising from the infinite ocean of Love that is the presence of God. I am a wave that has arisen from the ocean of my Father's holy mind. And though two waves seem to appear separated by what is called time—by

Lesson 4: *Following the Thread of Desire*

even two thousand of your years—when seen from a much broader perspective, those waves have arisen simultaneously from the ocean's surface. They arise for the very same purpose: to express the simplicity, the innocence, the beauty, the creativity, the truth and the reality of the ocean itself.

The waves delight in expressing what seems to be a unique individuality. Yet, they carry the common thread of being made of the same substance and are truly governed by the same laws of creation.

They know not the moment of their own arising, for only the depth of the ocean unseen can know the moment when it chooses to well up and to create the expression of the wave. The power that is not seen, but is hidden in the depth of the ocean rises up and forms that wave, and sustains it throughout the duration of its expression. It is from the depth of that ocean that it is decided when that wave shall return to the sea.

Does that mean it disappears? Only from one perspective. But in reality, the very substance that was made manifest truly has not known birth and death, but only expression.

What if you were to consider *yourself* as a wave arising from the holy Mind of God, born of God's infinite desire to expand Herself, to express the infinite nature of Love and creativity? What if you began to realize that all that you have called yourself is the *effect* of Love—that you did not *cause* yourself to come into existence?

And yet, as you have arisen from that ocean of Love, is not the wave made of the same substance as the sea itself? Are you not given infinite and perfect freedom? For just as your Father perceives you, you are given the freedom to perceive yourself, and all of the other waves you might notice, even the ocean itself, in any way that you choose.

The goal, then, of genuine spirituality is to realign the quality of your perception—to mirror, to resonate with, to be in perfect alignment with the perception of your Creator—to see with God's eyes. Beloved friends, in truth, you remain as you were created to be. This means that in each and every moment, you are literally using the power found in the silent depth of the ocean of God's Love that gave rise to your very creation and existence to perceive as you desire.

Lesson 4: *Following the Thread of Desire*

Therefore, in this lesson, we will address the very nature of desire itself. We will address what it means, what it signifies and how it creates effects. We will address the power of desire, the value of desire, the meaning and purpose of desire, and how to begin to bring that energy—which at times feels like a team of a thousand wild horses all wanting to go in their own directions—under your conscious and deliberate direction. So that you might create as the Father created you—with perfect, deliberate and infinite Love, with perfect, infinite and deliberate joy, and with perfect—*perfect*—freedom.

Desire! When I walked upon your planet as a man, I confronted many different opinions about the nature of creation, the nature of humankind, and the nature of consciousness or self-identity. Just as you are now confronted with many schools of thought, so too was I. While that can seem to lead to great confusion, as though one must choose from the smorgasbord, it actually serves not unlike the sand inside the oyster from which the pearl will come. It causes you to grate inside.

You must find your own way to your own truth. For before each and every one of you lies your pathway, a doorway, an eye of the needle, through which *only you* can fit.

Therefore, in some respects, you are seemingly alone. You must make the decision to desire—above all things—awakening into perfect remembrance of your union with God. Just as a wave might finally decide that it has been birthed not to be fearful of being a wave, but to truly claim its individuation, its uniqueness and to live that fully. And in that fullness, it decides to discover a way to be aware of its infinite union with the ocean itself. It decides to somehow break free of the myopic self-identification as one little piece of wave that arises in a place or a field of time that lasts for but a second, and then disappears.

Just like the wave, you can decide to find a way to transcend limitation, to become re-identified with a consciousness, a living awareness that you are one with the depth of the sea. Decide that you can operate not from the superficial level of awareness that might be like the foam at the tip of the wave—which you call your conscious or egoic mind—but that you can become *in*formed in all that you speak, in all that you do, in all that you create, and all that

Lesson 4: *Following the Thread of Desire*

you perceive by that which rests in the very infinite depth of the ocean itself.

Imagine, then, drawing upon a well within you that seems to have no bottom and sides, through which something is pouring forth from places unseen, in which your literal conscious attention or awareness seems to be colored with radiant light. A light that literally leaves you feeling that you are not the body-mind or the personal history with which you had identified before. And an awareness that these things are only temporary and very impersonal effects of a level of desire within your soul, which is one and the same thing as the Love of God expressing Itself, for no other reason than that Love must be extended.

Imagine transcending your fear of your own survival because as you look upon your body-mind, you are no longer identified as that body-mind. It has become a tool to be utilized by the Love that rests in the Mind of God. You live, yet no longer you, but Christ dwells as you. *This is a very real experience to be lived.* It is not just a philosophy. It is not just a concept, and it can never be a dogma. There is a mystical translation that occurs in the depth of the soul, which is merely a shifting of where you

The Way of the Heart

perceive your sense and source of identity.

What is the energy required to take you from myopic self-contraction, in which you have become identified with the little drops of foam out on the tip of the wave that are tossed to and fro by a power that seems to be outside of you, to a sense of identity with the silent depth of the ocean that is everywhere present and seems to know no beginning or no end? The very energy that will carry you from the tip of the wave to the depth of the ocean is the energy of desire.

For I say unto you, if God had not desired to extend Love, you would never have come into existence. Your very sense of awareness of self is the result or the effect of Love. It is the very same Love that has birthed the sun and the moon and all of the stars and every dimension upon dimension upon dimension of creation. That very Love that desired to be extended is the very Source from which you have been birthed. As you know yourself to be, you are the effect of God's desire to extend Love.

When next someone asks you, "Who are you?" please do not give them a name. Do not say,

Lesson 4: *Following the Thread of Desire*

"Well, I was born in a certain town in a certain part of the planet." Do not tell them that you are a democrat, or a republican, or a communist, or an atheist or a catholic. Tell them the truth:

> Who am I? I am the extension of Love in form.
> I have never been born and I will never taste death.
> I am infinite and eternal.
> I shine forth as a sunbeam to the sun.
> I am the effect of God's Love.
> And I stand before you to love you.

Now *that* will raise some eyebrows! It will also transform your world. For it is time to stop seeking Christ outside and start choosing to take responsibility for being Christ incarnate.

Desire Is Everything

Take a moment right now and let the body relax. Imagine that you can move back from being the actor in the play of your life to being the director and the producer. You are sitting in your studio, and you are editing the story of your life. You are looking at all your little clips of film. Clips from the time you were birthed, the time you went to kindergarten, the time you first fell in love, the time you first decided to go to a movie, the time you went off to college. Or the time you took a job, this job or that job, or the time you moved to another physical location.

Look closely and see if it is not true that for every action you have ever done, for every decision you have ever made, after trying to analyze it all, is there not underneath it the energy of desire?

In truth, you do not lift the body from your couch to go to the refrigerator without the desire to eat. Something calls you into an expression of action. It is desire. No one enters into an intimate relationship without the energy of desire. For what two have ever looked upon one another and said, "I don't feel any desire whatsoever, but let's get married, have children, and raise a family?"

Desire is that energy which brings forth all waves of creation out of the depth of the ocean itself. And yet, who among you has not felt conflicted about desire? Who among you has not been taught that desire is evil? Who among you has not been taught not to desire to be great? Who

LESSON 4: *Following the Thread of Desire*

among you has not been taught that the desire for material comfort is some sort of a blot on the spiritual path? Look well within your soul and see if this is not true.

Have you not feared, at times, the welling up of desire within you? For as I look upon your plane, there are many who become paralyzed with fear just because they desire to have a bowl of ice cream. So afraid are they that if they give in to that desire, something in the ice cream will cause their body to bloat and their brain to cease functioning!

For those of you in intimate relationship—marriage or a commitment of some kind—how many of you have not carried the belief, taught to you by the world, that if you feel an energy of desire welling up within you when you look upon someone who is not your partner, somehow you have sinned against God? How many of you do not know the experience of trying to reign in the ten thousand horses, so sure that if you gave in to feeling desire, that everything would run amuck? And that your attempt to keep your life structured, rigid and predictable would collapse, and "all hell would break loose!"

Yet I say unto you, would you exist if God had feared the desire to create and extend Love by forming *you*, at the same time giving you infinite freedom of choice? Without desire—look around—not only would you see nothing, there would be nothing to do the seeing. *Everything* is the *effect* of desire.

Come then to see that desire is not evil. It is *not* to be feared. It is to be mastered. Mastery is not control. For control—the need to control—is an effect of the energy of fear, not Love. Mastery of desire comes when you recognize that you are safe to feel whatever wave of desire might come up through your consciousness, because *you* decide whether or not you will act on it, whether you will bring it into the field of manifestation.

The power of choice is the one power that can never be taken from you. You already have perfect mastery of it, because nothing you ever experience comes to you without your decision to allow it into the field of manifestation.

Desire is something that wells up from the depth beyond yourself that can be looked at with perfect innocence, and with the wonder of a child.

Lesson 4: *Following the Thread of Desire*

The very act of turning to allow and welcome desire is not something that will sidetrack you from the path of awakening, but will take you vertically into the Heart of God. For if you are to ever create as God creates, you will need to heal your conflicted perceptions about desire. You will need to transcend that energy of fear.

There are many who call unto me and pray. There is not an hour in your time frame in which there are not many upon your plane, somewhere on your planet, who are praying to me and want their hearts to be filled with Christ. Yet, at the very same time, they are scared to death of an energy that *wants* to move, because they have been taught to fear and to suppress desire.

Desire is like the liquid of life that moves through the stem of the rose and allows the petals to radiate with glorious color. When you block the flow of desire, the petals cannot be nourished. Death begins to occur—death of the heart, death of the soul and lifelessness.

If you were to walk down one of your city streets and to truly look into the eyes of everyone you see, would you not recognize that death seems to have already made a home in the minds of many that are living? Death of dreams, death of hope, death of worthiness, death of playfulness, death of true power and death of union with their Source and Creator has already taken place. Everyone who reads these words has had this experience of seeing this in others.

Healing requires the willingness to feel desire, to see it as good and to see it as holy. Does that not mean that if you feel a desire, that it might not become twisted by the egoic patterns in your mind? Of course not. There is always the possibility that desire will be twisted to meet the needs of the egoic mind within you. But rest assured, if it does, who has done it? You! Always within you, you have known that desire is good, but you suppressed it. Those times when desire came forth and you let it become twisted into serving the goals of the ego, you always knew perfectly well what you were doing. You were the decision-maker.

You have learned, therefore, to fear desire because that fear is the effect of fearing yourself, and that is what cripples you. That is what cuts off the creative flow. That is what leads to every-

LESSON 4: *Following the Thread of Desire*

thing your world knows as the multitude of psychological dis-eases: an unwillingness to trust one's self, an unwillingness to love one's self and the belief that the desires that move up through your beingness are something evil and dark.

You think that if only you could stamp them out of your being, you could remain in control and everybody would like you because you would conform to the smallness and the littleness that is worshiped in human consciousness.

Understand well the next axiom we give to you:

> The only relationship that holds any value
> at all is your relationship with God, your
> creative Source, the depth of the ocean.

Right away the mind says, "But what about my mate, what about my parents, what about my children, what about the president of the United States, what about the postmaster?" You will come up with a million examples of relationships that surely have great importance.

The *only* one that holds value is your relationship with God. For when that is in alignment, all of your creations, your choices for relationships and how you will be within them will flow effortlessly *from* that alignment. Therefore, seek first the Kingdom, and all these things will be added unto you. Do not try to create a rose by starting with the petals, but nourish the roots, and the flower must blossom.

If you are to be in right relationship with your Creator, it is absolutely necessary to correct your perception and relationship with the energy of desire. It begins by releasing your judgment of it in all of its forms. For again, you can only be in Love or fear. You can only be in innocence or judgment. Love and innocence are of the Kingdom. Fear and judgment are of illusion.

Releasing Judgment of Desire

Learn then, through simple practice, to interrupt the patterns you have learned from this illusory world, so that you release judgment of the energy of desire. This will be different for each and every one, depending on where you begin.

Here is a very simple exercise. When you awaken in the morning and you have planted your feet firmly on your floor, take pause and ask yourself this question:

LESSON 4: *Following the Thread of Desire*

What do I want right now?

Right away, the mind will say, "Well, I'm too busy to know what I want, I have to go off to work. I have to serve everybody else. I'm here to satisfy the world. I have no time to ask *myself* what I want."

Remember that what you decree is, and the thought you hold in the mind will be reflected through the nature of your experience.

So take pause and ask, "What do I want?" Then simply give yourself one minute to observe whatever comes up in the mind, or even is felt in the body.

Heaven forbid, you might want to have sex! Oh! Then you would know for sure that you are not a "spiritual" being!

You might want to take a hot shower. You might want a glass of juice or water. You might want to sing. You might want to stretch or breathe. You might want to turn and look at your lover, your mate, still sleeping in the bed. You might want to arise, and sneak into your children's room and watch them sleep. You might want to sit down and read the morning paper.

The point here is to notice that by asking the question, something will respond within you. And when that response comes, notice that there is a feeling associated with it, a quality that makes your cells sing just a little bit. That is the energy, the elixir of life, called desire.

In this one minute, you need not rise to act, but to simply observe: "Ah, what do I want? To take a hot shower." The feeling of the thought, or the thought that emits the feeling in the body, "I want to take a hot shower," is carried on the elixir of desire.

Desire is coming from a depth of your being that, again, rests right next to the face of God. Might it not be the case that by following the desire that wells up through your heart, by feeling it, by embracing it, you might learn and discover what the ocean is wishing to express through the wave that you are? If you judge desire, might you not be shutting off the creative flow that the Mind of God wishes to express?

Of course, that is the problem. You have tied the hose in a knot through conflicted judgments. Here is a very common one in your world. Be honest with yourself, how many times have you

Lesson 4: *Following the Thread of Desire*

felt the desire to be wealthy? It is not something you are supposed to sit around and talk about or make very public, especially if you are trying to be "spiritual."

You may have thought, "I woke up this morning and I just imagined having so many golden coins that I could buy the entire planet!" Then you remembered, "Oh! 'Money is the root of all evil.' I can't think that way. Well, I better get busy and get off to my office job, that secretly inside I really resent because they don't pay me what my soul is worth. But I'll pretend like I'm quite fine. Oh, money? No, I'm quite fine. I really have enough. No, no, I'm really quite fine."

Then as you drive home and a Mercedes pulls up alongside you, you cannot help but turn and say, "God, I wish I could afford one of those." Then you think, "Oh, God! I can't have that thought, so I'll just drive my old Volkswagen down the road. But I'm being a very good spiritual person."

Be honest with yourself. How many times have you felt welling up within you the desire to be wealthy? What on earth has caused you to fear that desire? What has caused you to tie the hose in a knot, so that you try to block that desire from coming into manifestation?

Perhaps when you were a child, you went to one of your cathedrals. And there was someone in a long robe standing upon a platform and because everything looked so beautiful, you thought that surely they must have been speaking with authority. Since this cathedral was filled with a whole lot of small little minds that were all living in their own level of fear, they said, "Money is the root of all evil." And you thought, "Oh, well, that is the truth. Oh, yes, that's the truth. Oh, God! I better fear money."

I say unto you, you have one authority, and it is never held within the office of any church, or any organization or any one individual. Your authority is the voice for God that dwells within your heart and within your mind! God is not limited, and does not require His children to be limited. For if you would receive all that God would give you, you must decide to rise up and be the grandest wave that you could possibly be. For only in so doing, do you honor your Creator.

You could say that God is like a wise gardener who is constantly trying to grow beautiful roses.

LESSON 4: *Following the Thread of Desire*

She knows exactly how much moisture to put in the soil. She knows how to make those nutrients rise from the soil through the roots, up through the heart of the stem of the flower to give forth radiant color, so that everyone that looks upon it is touched by the mystery of beauty.

And God wonders, "Well, it is interesting. These roses that I have created seem to have a mind of their own. As the elixir I tried to give them rises through the stems, they tie themselves in little knots and only a little bit of the elixir reaches out. So the petals never quite blossom fully."

Have you ever had that feeling that you are putting more energy into staying constricted than you are into allowing expansion?

Desire Links You to the Will of God

Desire is creation. Therefore, *what* you desire is of supreme importance. If you will take the little exercise that we have given you and begin to put it into practice upon awakening in the morning, in a very simple and quiet way, you will begin to get back in touch with the innocence and beauty of the movement of desire. You can delight in it.

When you have a sexual thought, a sexual desire, why not just be with it? Why not notice what it causes to happen in the body? How does your breath change? Does the heart beat faster? Be honest with yourself, is it not putting a smile on your face? What if you decided to honestly embrace that effect as being perfectly innocent and beautiful? How might your day change if you did not repress awareness of sexual desire?

You will notice we are not saying you should walk down the street and grab every body that walks by you. We are talking about allowing yourself the living embrace of exactly what energy is moving through your being.

Why is this important? If you have decided that there are certain energies that are demonic, evil or have the power to distract you from your union with God, you have already decided there is something *beyond* the reach of your power. And that is what dis-empowers you. You take an innocent energy and turn it into a monster that must be feared at all cost.

Yet I say this unto you. The mystical transformation that carries you from feeling yourself to be a disem-

Lesson 4: *Following the Thread of Desire*

powered little drop of foam on the edge of a wave to the sense of freedom and empowered living that flows from the Mind of God through you to express only beautiful creations filled with majesty, power and miracles is *willingness*. The willingness to turn to the very energies that move through the mind and the body and to not fear them. But instead to look upon them with innocence and wonder.

This is the source of the myths that have been told in all cultures: the knight that slays the dragon or kissing the wild beast on the cheek and it becomes a loving companion. Your monsters are what you fear and repress because of the judgments you have learned in the world. And the world is only the denial of the Kingdom. It is the exact opposite of Truth.

If you are sitting in one of your cathedrals and everyone is saying, "Sexuality is very bad! It will keep you from God." Right away, you should realize if everyone here fears sexuality, it must actually be divine. Allow yourself to think, "Perhaps I would do well to embrace it, love it, master it and not fear it."

Imagine someone says unto you, "Money is the

root of all evil!" and then puts out his hand and says, "Would you please make a donation to our organization?" Is that not an expression of conflict? Yet such conflict permeates the religions and dogmas of your world, which say, "Don't desire money. Don't desire wealth. By the way, to keep the ministry on this radio station, we really need you to send a donation." What are they trying to teach you? What are they in denial of?

Sex and money. Pretty basic things, are they not? They represent energies that flow from the Mind of God, which would express in unlimited joy and power, and not be willing to settle for limitation of any kind.

When the Earth was birthed from God's holy Mind and took on its own form and became an entity just like you, God did not say, "Well, this is a pretty beautiful planet, but I can only have a solar system just large enough for the Earth." Rather, out of joy, God allowed there to come forth solar system upon solar system upon solar system, the birthing of a thousand suns every moment, as a field in which this beautiful jewel of a planet could spin. *That* is true creation! What quality of solar system have *you* decided to allow,

LESSON 4: *Following the Thread of Desire*

in which the planet of your own awareness can spin and live and express?

Desire is everything. The simple exercise we have given you will begin to free up the blocks within, and you will rediscover the innocence of desire. Then you can begin to expand upon it, to take a few moments to learn to live deliberately, asking yourself, "What do I *truly* want?" Use your consciousness to relax into the innocence of the question:

> What do I truly want?
> What is it in my heart that keeps calling
> to me, keeps compelling me?

Because your mind shines forth like a sunbeam to the sun from the Mind of God, when you ask the question, pictures will begin to arise, feelings will begin to arise. And I say unto you, they are symbols and expressions of what God wants to bring forth *through* you.

You may say, "Every time I look in my heart, and every time I allow myself to feel it, what I really want is to put my arms around people. I want to let people know how much I love them." Why fear such a desire? Do you say, "It's too overwhelming. I don't know how I'll be accepted."

Who cares how you will be accepted?
What matters is how you accept yourself.

What if by feeling that desire, new pictures began to come to you? For example, suddenly you realized, "What I want to do is join the Peace Corps." Perhaps that very decision would be like putting yourself in a solar system where you can spin as your own planet. What if going and being in the Peace Corps could be the very pathway through which you learn to receive the great joy of letting your love out to the world? But if you fear desire, how can you ever know these things?

What comes up for you by asking that question? It might be, "I want to have so much wealth." And I see the thought that says, "Oh, no, wealth is bad." But if you allow yourself to continue to ask the question, a deeper answer will emerge, such as, "What I want is to be able to go to all the hungry children on the planet and feed them. That's why I want to be wealthy."

Could it not be that the desire to feed the world is God's desire to speak through you, to use you in a

Lesson 4: *Following the Thread of Desire*

way that effects transformation upon your planet? Can you see that by blocking the feeling of desire, you might just be blocking yourself from hearing what you keep praying for over and over? You pray, "Father, reveal thy purpose to me." Then you feel the desire and say, "Oops! Excuse me, Father. I have to get rid of this desire first."

Desire in the heart is where you will discover the phone line that links you to the will of God that would be expressed through you. If you do not trust desire, you are literally saying that you have decided not to trust your Creator. That is a statement not just to be brushed aside. In healing the conflict around desire, now that you know what it truly is, learn to be patient with yourself.

An Exercise in Trusting Desire

We would suggest that you create a structure by which a second exercise can be practiced that fits into your life. Again, it need not take more than five, ten or fifteen minutes initially, perhaps three or four times a week. Eventually, you will be doing this all the time because you will be creating deliberately. For just ten or fifteen minutes, set aside your world. Remember that you need do nothing, so the world can wait.

Relax the body and close the eyes. It can be of great benefit to let the breath become very deep and rhythmic. It relaxes the nervous system and seduces the controller within your mind—the critic that decides what thoughts are acceptable and which ones are not. By the way, the critic is never something you created. It is something you let live in your mind that was made up by a lot of other fearful minds, called parents and teachers.

As you relax the body and the mind, ask yourself:

What do I truly want?

Observe the images that come, without judgment. Notice the feelings in the body, and allow this to go on for just a minute or two. Then pause, open the eyes, and write down all that you can remember. For example, "I saw the image of having forty-seven sexual partners. I saw the image of having golden coins rain down upon me so that I had to have an umbrella over my head. I saw huge bowls of ice cream. I saw myself in a boat on the ocean. I notice that my stomach got tight." Whatever it is, write it down.

Then, take a deep breath, relax again, and repeat

LESSON 4: *Following the Thread of Desire*

the process. Place the hand so that it rests on the heart. Breathe into it a few times, and then ask,

What do I truly desire?

Again, allow the process to be what it is. Do this over a period of ten or fifteen minutes so that you repeat the process at least six or seven times, writing everything down.

Then take the piece of paper or journal and put it aside until the next exercise period, and again repeat the process. When you have done this seven times, so that you have seven sheets of paper in which you have gone through this process, then, and only then, begin to look back through all the things that came up. Ask yourself, "What seems to be repeating itself?" You might notice that three times you wanted a huge bowl of ice cream, but then it seemed to fade away. Twice you had a desire for forty-seven lovers, but now you notice that you are really only wanting one.

Whatever it might be, notice the pattern, the thread that seems to run the most throughout the exercise periods. Then, imagine that thread to be the energetic link that is tied at one end to the piece of foam at the edge of the wave, and the

The Way of the Heart

other is anchored to the depth of the ocean. Then consider that, perhaps, if you allowed yourself to move down that thread, to begin to put your energy on that, to begin to clear up the obstacles within your consciousness that block that desire from being consistently lived from, you would carry yourself from the drop of foam at the edge of the wave to the Heart of God.

And along the way, everything unlike Love would come up for you to release it. During the process, you would go through a metamorphosis that would culminate in your being the living incarnation of the power of Christ—your soul would realize the fulfillment that it has always sought.

For you see, the reason you have cleverly decided to trick yourself into blocking the energy of desire is that the soul knows that were it to follow such a thread through whole and total commitment, it will be embarking on the pathway set before you by God that knows how to take you home.

If you arrive at home, it will mean that you will have had to give up being a *seeker*. You will have had to become one who has *found*. And you will have to rise above the crowd. You will have to

Lesson 4: *Following the Thread of Desire*

give up all of your identity with smallness. You will have to give up needing the approval of others. You will have left the nest of insanity. You will have arisen and taken up your rightful place at the right hand of God. Is not that the deepest fear you carry—to actually be the Truth of who you are: Christ incarnate?

Desire can be much fun. Ideally, once you have practiced this on your own, ask your mate or a close friend if they would be willing to embark on this process with you, so that perhaps once a week you can sit down together and say, "What did you come up with this week?"

It is called undressing in front of a friend. It is called becoming vulnerable with another. It is called finding another child to play with in the Kingdom, so that you can go to the sandbox, away from the adult world that says, "Desire is bad. You guys be careful."

You begin to look at what is true and real from a place of innocence. You begin to create for yourself a support group. And that support group perhaps can grow to three or four friends—or even ten or twenty—in which everyone is

The Way of the Heart

involved with getting in touch with what is really in there, by understanding the principle that desire is the thread that links your soul to the Heart of God. And God wants only to extend, through you, that which expresses Love in the world. It is called creation.

Perhaps, it is a worthwhile project. For when you do not turn to allow the embrace of desire, there is only one alternative. It is to live in mere survival. When you choose the energy of mere survival, the *world* is your master, before which you will be made to bow again and again and again and again and again, lifetime after lifetime after lifetime! You will be a *slave* to the insanity that seems to rule this world.

And you will never know peace. You will never know joy. And you will never come home. Plain and simple! But you were not created to wither and die on the vine. You were made to bear forth much good fruit.

Let the roots be watered by desiring, above all things, to become the fulfillment of what God had in mind when He breathed into you the breath of Life. Let that breath be received in each moment. You will come to see that the *only*

Lesson 4: *Following the Thread of Desire*

question—the only question—you need be preoccupied with is this:

> How much of God am I willing to receive and allow to be expressed through me?

It is called "separating the wheat from the chaff." The chaff is the thinking of the world that would have you believe in smallness. This can only result in your perpetual suffering. The wheat is the food that gives life, because it is filled with the Love of God.

Fear not, then, desire. But desire to embrace desire. Touch it, feel it, know it, dance with it, sing with it, and look at it innocently. Feel it wholly. And then learn to discern, through the ways we have given you, what desire is truly: that thread that is shining forth through all of your days. Then decide to let that desire *in*form your choices, so that you create a life that serves the fulfillment of that thread of desire.

I had to do the same. For I began to notice that there was a thread of desire in my heart to create some form of demonstration that would be so overwhelming that *anyone* who turned their attention to it could not help but be reminded that there is something far greater to life than living to survive, and surviving just to live. Even when I was young, I began to get glimpses. At first, they were fleeting. Something was compelling me, and as I learned to trust desire, the pictures became clearer and clearer.

In those moments of revelation when I was still but a teenager, I saw myself standing on hilltops, surrounded by multitudes. And I marveled at the words that came through my mouth. I saw glimpses and pictures of being loved by millions. I saw pictures and things that I could not even comprehend, because they were literally pictures of what I am doing *now*. And how could a teenager, living in Judea two thousand years ago, have any way of comprehending the use of the technologies of your modern world in which to communicate Love? It made no sense to me. But still, I decided to trust it.

A part of that thread was the recognition that death is unreal. Therefore, I thought that I ought to be able to create a demonstration that would prove it. Now, think about that for a moment! If that thought was born in you, and you tried to

Lesson 4: *Following the Thread of Desire*

share it with the world, would you not be told you were crazy to dare to think a thought so out of line with everything the world believes? But because I followed the thread of desire, I began to realize that it kept speaking to me, day after day, and week after week. It wanted to grow. It wanted to be nurtured. Finally, I decided:

> I am going to allow that thread to be nurtured.
> I am going to discover where it takes me,
> and what it is all about.

Where it took me was into mastery of life and death, mastery of healing, mastery of consciousness. It took me into mastery of myself. It brought me home to my own Christed beingness.

Because I followed that thread, I can talk with you today. There are many of you that appreciate what I have done, because you see me as a spokesperson for the Truth. Is it not time that *you* followed your own thread, and became, likewise, a spokesperson for reality? For just as you have been sent to me, there will be many sent to you, as you step from being a seeker to a finder. For as you take up your rightful place, you become a vehicle through which the voice for God will creatively touch the lives of countless persons that you may never ever meet physically.

You were birthed to be grand. You were birthed for greatness. You were birthed to shine forth such light into this world that the world remembers that light is true, and darkness is illusion. Be you, therefore, that which you are—you are the light of the world. And I will delight in journeying with you. I can join with anyone who chooses to step into their own Christedness. The connecting thread is the thread of desire.

Therefore, begin to turn toward the energy of desire within yourself—to separate the wheat from the chaff—by first learning to feel it for just a minute without judging it, and then to deepen that process. You will reach the point where with every breath that you breathe, you are in touch with the energy of desire. And that is the only voice that you will give authority to.

You will not be able to keep up with the loving creation that wants to express through you. You will marvel at the friends that come into your life and how your external solar system, in which your planet is spinning, changes. You will marvel

LESSON 4: *Following the Thread of Desire*

and wonder how it is all happening. You will finally discover that you are not the maker and doer of your life, that God wants to direct and make Life *through you*. Then you will know the Truth that sets you free:

> Of myself, I do nothing.
> But my Father, through me, does all things.
> And it is very good.

Be you, therefore, at peace. And desire well. For when you feel desire, you are watering your roots with the energy of Life itself. Trust it! Embrace it! And let the petals of the rose *blossom* within your holy being.

We love you, and we are with you. If you could only see how much enlightened help there is surrounding you at any moment, you would never allow the fear of going astray with your desire to be victorious within your mind. You would step forth with boldness. And all things would be made new again.

> How much of God's Love are you
> willing to receive? Amen.

Lesson 5

The Keys to the Kingdom

Beloved friends, we come forth in this lesson to continue that pathway which builds the structure, the highway by which you may learn to follow and, therefore, master The Way of the Heart. A *way* in life means to have chosen from all possibilities that one which will stand out as the way to which you are committed, the way to which you devote the whole of your attention by granting your willingness that the way be followed. Just as when you take a journey upon your Earth by making the commitment to take the journey, you avail yourselves of experiences that could not come to you in any other way.

When you go to a university to pursue a degree, although you begin with a certain idea of what the pathway may hold or bring you, is it not true that the relationships which come along the way, the knowledge that reveals itself to you, and

Lesson 5: *The Keys to the Kingdom*

even the end result of accomplishing the degree always seems to be different and much richer than you could have imagined when you began your journey?

Therefore, understand well that The Way of the Heart requires the willingness to commit. Commitment is nothing more than a deliberate decision that something will be so. Just as with all aspects of experience you have ever known, when all of your being is involved in the willingness to make a decision, there is literally nothing that can prevent you from the accomplishment of your goal.

Rest assured, whenever you believe you have not succeeded or not completed some decision fueled by desire, it is because you were simply not wholly committed—or you decided to change your mind. And when you change your mind, you literally change what you experience in the world or the solar system in which your *self* spins.

The Way of the Heart, then, does indeed require the decision of commitment. I say unto you that when you wholly commit to discovering The Way of the Heart, you will discover a way of being in the world that is not here. You will discover a way of walking through life in which you experience being uplifted by something that seems to be forever beyond you, yet is within you as the core and the essence of your very being.

Your way will not be understandable by the world. Your way will not even be comprehensible within yourself. You will be living from mystery—moving from mystery to mystery to mystery—uplifted and carried by something that brings a satisfaction and a fulfillment to the depth of your soul, far beyond anything you can now imagine.

Is it worth it to commit to The Way of the Heart? Yes! It culminates with the recognition that you do not live Life at all, but rather that Life is living you. One of its characteristics is the development of the witness—a quality of consciousness, a way of being—in which you seem to be witnessing everything that arises and flows through you and around you from a place of utter stillness.

Stillness does not mean non-activity. It does mean non-attachment to activity—whether it be the

Lesson 5: *The Keys to the Kingdom*

arising and falling away of cancer in the body, the arising and falling away of relationship, or the rising and falling away of a solar system.

You will discover that there is a place within you that can look upon all things with perfect equanimity, perfect acceptance, and perfect Love. For in mastery of The Way of the Heart, you will discover that nothing is unacceptable to you. Only what is accepted can be transcended.

You will discover a way of being in which nothing any longer compels you—not even the desire to know God compels you any longer, for the need of it has been completed.

Then there arises a way of being in the world that is indeed not here, for you will feel no restlessness, no need to direct your journey. No questions will arise. You will be at peace. In that peace, the breath of God will move through you. And you will become as the wind, knowing not where you came from or where you are going, but you will abide in perfect trust and perfect rest. The world may not know you, but your Father will know you—and *you* will know your God.

In The Way of the Heart, the most primary and

fundamental perception that seems to fuel ordinary human consciousness has been finally transcended. The perception of a separate "maker and doer" has been dissolved, and once again you will understand the depth and the profundity of the simple terms in this sentence:

> Of myself, I do nothing. But through me,
> the Father does all things.

To rest in such a perception means that you have come to realize that the self that you are is merely a conduit, through which mystery lives itself, through which Love pours forth. You will realize that there is nothing to be gained or lost in this world. You will know what it means to recognize that you literally have nowhere to go and nothing to achieve. You will become empty and spacious.

And yet paradoxically, while the body lasts, you will appear to be as everyone else. You will arise in the morning and brush your teeth. When the body is hungry, you will feed it. You will laugh with your friends. You will yawn when the body is a bit tired. Yet through it all, there will be a quality of awareness—called the witness—that is simply watching it all, waiting to be moved by

LESSON 5: *The Keys to the Kingdom*

the wind of Spirit. Though others may not see it, virtually everything you utter will carry the sound of truth.

You will not know how Spirit will work through you, nor will you care. Because, you see, when there is no maker or doer or director, it will not matter to you. That is what it means to live as the wind, for the wind does not concern itself with where it has been or where it is going. It is moved by some mysterious source that cannot be located at all. Yet it blows, and as it blows, its effect is experienced.

Imagine then a life in which all that you do is not *for* yourself. Imagine a way of life in which what you do is not *for* anyone else. Imagine a way of life in which creativity flows forth from a Source so deep within you and around you that no language or dogma can contain it—a force and a Source that knows how to express itself through you in such a way that it is constantly and only serving the atonement, the awakening of all of creation to the truth of God's presence.

The Way of the Heart does, indeed, unfold along a certain pathway. In this lesson, we will address the stages of that pathway, in a general sense.

Then we will speak of the most important characteristic to be cultivated along this path.

The First Key Is Desire

First, desire is everything. Without it, not a thing can arise. Therefore, *what* you desire is of utmost importance. Desire, then, perfect union with God. Desire, then, to be Christ incarnate. Desire, then, to be all that your Creator has created you to be, even if you have no idea what that might be.

For when you hold desire within your beingness and when you have mastered the energy of desire—again, mastery does not mean control—by grounding it always in the desire to be as you are created to be, then indeed all of your life and all of the subsequent or subsidiary desires will come to serve that grand desire.

When you come into that state of being, nothing shall be impossible unto you. Why? Because you are not the one doing it. You are ~~merely~~ a piece of thread in a very cosmic tapestry being woven by the Creator of all of creation, who alone knows how to weave the tapestry of a new age, of a new paradigm, of a healing of this plane and of humanity.

So the first stage is the stage of desire. Only by feeling desire and not by suppressing it can you truly begin to move toward the stage of mastery in which the energy of desire always serves that higher will, which is the will of God for you. As we have said to you before, when your will is in alignment with the will of God, you will discover that God's will for you is that you be genuinely happy through and through, content, fulfilled, at peace, empowered, capable, and responsible.

The Second Key Is Intention

Desire, in time, is cultivated through *intention*. For you have used time to teach yourself how to be distracted by all of the thoughts and perceptions that make up this cosmic soup called your world. All of you have known the frustration of having a desire, and then as soon as you walk out the door a friend pulls up and says, "Let's go to the beach." And you never make it to class, even though your desire is to get the degree. You have cultivated the art of being seduced by distraction.

Therefore, it is necessary to utilize time to cultivate intention. For without intention, desire cannot become the crystal clear focus, the laser-like focus that can cut through the dross of this world so that a new creation can flow forth through you.

Intention is not the same as holding a strong egoic or willed commitment to making something happen. For The Way of the Heart recognizes that you have not known how to achieve the fulfillment you seek at the level of the soul, for the simple reason that if you did, you would have already accomplished it. Intention does not mean putting your nose to the grindstone and not taking "no" for an answer.

Rather, it means that you cultivate within your thought processes the art of remembering what you are truly here for. You are here to remember that you are the thought of Love in form. You are here to remember that you are one with God. You are here to remember that what I have called Abba, though it goes by many names, is the source of your only reality. You are living in reality only to the degree that That One is living through you.

Therefore, intention in The Way of the Heart means to utilize time each day to focus your attention on the desire to be Christ incarnate.

LESSON 5: *The Keys to the Kingdom*

Intention is that energy or that use of the mind that creates—through consistent practice—the channel through which desire begins to move down and re-educate the emotional body, and even the cellular structure of the physical body, and all of the lesser avenues of thinking that occur within the intellect. So everything involved in your being is integrated, working together and <u>focused</u> on the fulfillment of that one grand desire to accept your function in this world. Your function is healing your sense of separation from God.

How do you apply intention? Each day just as you have used time to teach yourself to be easily distracted, you need only ask yourself one question daily:

> What is it that I most desire?
> What am I doing on this planet?
> What am I committed to?

The last two questions are just forms of the fundamental question. As you keep practicing asking that question, the answer will become clearer and clearer. For it is the question that influences, stimulates, and gives birth to the answer. The universe is always answering your questions. And when you ask unclear questions, you get unclear answers. Therefore, become crystal clear with your intention and remind yourself of it daily:

- My intention is to use time constructively for the relearning of what it means to abide in the Kingdom of Heaven and to fulfill my function. My function is healing. And healing requires the presence of Christ, for only Christ can express the Love that brings healing into being.

Desire and intention are critical. These stages unfold in the field of time as one matures in The Way of the Heart.

The Third Key Is Allowance

The third stage of the process whereby the mind is wholly corrected and one returns home is the stage of allowance. For the egoic world does not teach you to allow, it teaches you to strive. *You* must be the maker and the doer. *You* must find a way to manipulate or control your environment in order that it conform itself to the image that you are holding in your mind.

Lesson 5: *The Keys to the Kingdom*

All of that is well and good, and there are many beings that learn some valuable lessons by following the path of certain teachers that will teach you that you can create whatever you want. That will seem like such a big deal until you realize it is what you are doing all of the time! You are always creating exactly what you decree. It is no big deal and it is not a secret.

But there will be those that will teach you, "Well, just go into your mind, ask yourself what you want, and when you see that picture of the Mercedes, then you simply do all of these little magical tricks and pretty soon, you end up with a Mercedes." The problem with that, although it can be a useful stage, is that the intellect, the worldly part of your mind, can only desire what it has been programmed to desire.

The worldly part of your mind says, "Well, I have to transport my body around in this plane. Automobiles do that. The world tells me that a Mercedes is a grand way of doing this, therefore, I will create the desire of wanting a Mercedes." When you manifest the Mercedes, you fool yourself into thinking that you have made great progress when, in fact, all you have done is done what you have always done. You have chosen what your experience will be and you have manifested it. There is nothing new about that. Although by so doing, you can begin to regain confidence in your ability to manifest.

The Way of the Heart is about something else. Allowance, in this pathway, means that you begin to view your life differently. It is not a struggle to get out of high school and create a career by which you can create golden coins, by which you can create the proper house in the proper environment so that your ego feels "successful" and, therefore, of being "worth" love.

Be honest with yourself—is not your world built on such premises as these: "If only I can make my life look successful around me, then I will be accepted, then I can love myself, at least a little. Maybe I can get other people to love me." That is not it at all.

The Way of the Heart begins with the recognition that you are *already* loved by the only Source that matters, that you have come for a much higher purpose that can be made manifest *in* the ways of the world, but is not *of* the world.

Lesson 5: *The Keys to the Kingdom*

Allowance is the cultivation of a way of looking at the events of your life, not as obstacles to getting what you want, but as stepping stones. Each one presents you with a blessing of the lessons required to heal the obstacles—not to success, but to the presence of Love as the Source and ground of your being.

In the stage of allowance, we begin to cultivate an acceptance of all things in our experience. We begin to see that because we have made a commitment to awakening and incarnating only Christ, the universe is already conspiring to bring the people and events into our lives, on a moment to moment basis, that can best provide us with exactly what we most need to learn or become aware of.

And so, messengers are sent. That messenger could come in the form of someone whom you fall in love with, and there is something there for you to learn. It could be that you have been blocking yourself from feeling love for other people, and now someone finally comes that blasts down the door and you cannot help but feel that feeling.

The messenger could be someone who comes as

the grain of sand within the oyster that causes the friction within you that nudges you from your sleep, and you realize that you have been operating out of some very dysfunctional patterns and that you have got to get a better grip upon the Truth of who you are.

It may be that you need to learn to express your feelings more. It may be that you need to accept your own creativity more. Through your messengers, that which causes you to finally be responsible and be honest about where you are will be brought up within you.

For instance, if you think, "Well, I never get angry anymore. After all, I'm a very spiritual person. I just got out of seminary and I know it all now. So, I'll just live in heavenly bliss." And events begin to happen. Perhaps, as an example, a gay couple moves into your neighborhood and you discover that you have some very deeply seated perceptions that there is something wrong with that sexual orientation. They are messengers, sent to you by the universe to push you to look more deeply.

Allowance, then, is the cultivation of a quality of awareness in which you rest in the recognition

LESSON 5: *The Keys to the Kingdom*

that your life is no longer your own to dictate and control. But that rather, you have given it over to the Source of your own beingness, to that depth of wisdom in the depth of the ocean that knows best how to bring about what is required to push up the dross from within your consciousness, so that you can release it.

Allowance cultivates trust. Allowance is the way in which intention and desire come to work ever more fully in the third dimension of your experience—the field of time. Allowance is a submission, but not a naive submission. Allowance changes your perception of what you see as the world around you.

You begin to realize that you do not really live in a real world at all. You live in a field of vibrations and energies that is operated by the law of attraction or resonance. And you begin to be willing to allow certain things to fall out of your life, even family and friends, trusting that because of your desire and intention, what passes out of your life must be okay. For it will be replaced by new vibrational patterns which come in the form of messengers—events, places, persons and things—that can carry you on the upward spiral of awakening.

• 143 •

Allowance means the beginning stages of the cultivation of humility and the recognition that you must finally submit to something beyond the intellect and the control of the egoic part of the mind because the maker and doer that has been trying to do it all is finally recognized as being inadequate.

The Fourth Key Is Surrender

As these three stages mature, you rest into the final stage of surrender. And surrender means there is no longer any restlessness. Surrender means you know through every fiber of your being that there is no one here living a life, there is Life flowing through the body-mind personality, for as long as it lasts.

Here is where the mystical transformation is culminated or completed. It is here that you understand the meaning of the teaching:

I live, yet not I, but Christ dwelleth as me.

Surrender is a stage in which perfect peace is the foundation, not for passivity or inactivity, but for even *more* activity.

You find yourself, as long as you are in the

LESSON 5: *The Keys to the Kingdom*

world, being busier and busier, and asked to do more and more. You become even more responsible. Eventually, you come to see that because you *are* Christ, you are responsible for the whole of creation. You come to see that you cannot think a thought without disturbing the farthest of stars. It is that responsibility from which you have shrunk and tried to contain yourself as a tiny myopic piece of foam, all because you have feared being responsible for the whole.

But The Way of the Heart corrects your perception so that you come to recognize that your greatest joy, your greatest fulfillment is in wholly and deliberately accepting responsibility for the whole of creation. Why? Because you suddenly realize you are not the maker and doer, that you can accept responsibility for anything and everything because through you all power under Heaven and Earth is made to flow, to manifest the Love of God. So, in short, it is in God's hands, not yours:

> Not my will, but Thine be done.

Does that begin to make sense to you? Do you see how it changes how you have even been taught to interpret my teachings?

Desire, intention, allowance, surrender. But it is a surrender into a way of being that the world can never know. It is surrender into a way of being in which you may never receive an Oscar for your acting. But it is a way of being in which your consciousness becomes totally open to your union with all of creation. You will talk with a leaf as it falls from a tree. You will see the soul of the kitten that you pet. You will talk with angels and masters. And you will be involved in board meetings in the high cosmic conference rooms.

You will know that the body-mind you once thought was yours is little more than a temporary teaching device, a tool to be picked up and utilized at God's direction, and put aside when its usefulness is done.

So that even when it is time to go through the transition that you know as death, nothing will disturb your peace. As the body dies—which means simply that your attention begins to release itself from it just like the hand of a carpenter is released from the handle of a hammer as it is laid down on the table on the way to dinner—you will be able to watch the process with total equanimity and joy.

Lesson 5: *The Keys to the Kingdom*

You will watch your Spirit disengage from the body. You will watch it crumble into lifelessness so that all of your attention becomes focused in a wholly new dimension. A dimension that is so vast that you will be able to look down upon the Earth plane, not unlike the way you might choose to hold a pebble in the palm of your hand. And in one quick glance, you see everything about the pebble and nothing is hidden.

I am one that has chosen to assume the responsibility for the pebble called Earth and all of life that dwells therein. You, too, will know that energy and reality of wrapping your fingers around the entirety of the solar system and becoming the god or the savior of that dimension. And it begins by choosing to take responsibility for your pebble, your domain, your solar system, your personal dimension. It begins by saying:

> I and I alone am the source of what
> I experience and perceive.
> I am not a victim of the world I see.
> Everything I experience, I have called to
> myself, plain and simple—no excuses, no
> ifs, ands, or buts. That is the way it is.

Gone will be your immaturity, your resistance to simply being responsible for your experience. The Way of the Heart then, cultivates a maturity of desire, intention, allowance, and surrender.

The Importance of Humility

No single characteristic is of greater importance than humility—not the feigned humility that is taught in certain world religions, but a *genuine* humility. For humility does not mean that you stand in front of a group of people who give you a standing ovation and say, "Oh, gosh! You don't have to do that. It's not important." So that you can look like you are humble when inwardly you are thinking, "Oh God, that feels so good! Clap a little louder, clap a little longer. But I won't tell you that." Do you know that kind of humility? Is it not the kind of humility you were taught in your schools?

Genuine humility flows from the deep-seated recognition that you cannot save yourself, that you are created and not Creator, that you are effect and not cause (in an absolute sense), that something called Life is not yours, that there is *something* beyond your capacity of containment and intellectual understanding. And if that something ever decided to give up loving you, you would cease to be.

No matter how deep you go into the depth of God, and no matter how deep you achieve an awareness and consciousness of union with God, what God is remains forever beyond your growing capacity to understand God. It is like an ocean of infinite depth. When you realize that strive as you might, you will never wrap your self, your little self, around that Source, you will rest into humility—genuine humility.

Why is this important? Mark these words well. As you progress along the path of The Way of the Heart, as you dissolve and loosen the shackles upon the mind, as the interior conflicts are healed and settled, as you begin to accept the abundance that the Father would bestow upon you in all levels of life and all levels of feeling and perception, as you begin to taste of the grandeur and the greatness that would flow through you, you will discover that the "enemies" become more subtle.

At a very immature, basic and naive level, every child views, at some stage, its parents as being its enemies, does it not? For example, the child says, "What do you mean I can't have the car tonight? What do you mean I must be home by 10:00 p.m.?" And the parent becomes the enemy.

As you move more and more into mastery, you will be sorely tempted to believe that you are done. You will be sorely tempted to believe, "I can do this. The prayers I used to do when I began, the simple exercises of awareness I used when I started my path, I don't need them anymore. I have mastered that." Any time you hear a voice within yourself saying, "I'm done," you may rest assured you are not. And you stand in danger of losing what you have gained.

Humility is the recognition that the more you move into mastery, the more there is the desire for discipline and vigilance. Discipline does not mean doing something hard that you do not like to do. Discipline is like the skill of an artist that cultivates and refines the skill, simply out of the deep desire and delight to create more beautifully. An athlete disciplines a muscle so that the muscle works even more beautifully than it did the day before, out of the sheer delight to extend greater beauty into the world.

LESSON 5: *The Keys to the Kingdom*

While you remain in existence, the creations of consciousness that are unlike Love have created a whole lot of vibratory patterns that would just love to pull you down. Therefore, the discipline of the mind that is required is to recognize that—while the body lasts—there can be a delight in consciously repeating the decision to teach only Love, selectively choosing only the vibrational patterns to be allowed into your consciousness that reflect the Truth and the beauty and the worthiness of who you truly are.

Judgment cannot reflect such light. Anger and hatred cannot do it. Fear and paranoia, fear of rejection, fear of the opinions of others and such vibrations can never reflect the regal grandeur of your being. Therefore, understand well that humility is absolutely essential. Paradoxically, as greatness is expressed through you, the temptation still will be to allow egoic energies to make a home in your mind. The ego's voice will say, "Boy, you are really quite a master, you know. You really deserve all this adulation. Why don't you keep ten percent of it for yourself?"

A master accepts the love and the gratitude offered by those whom his or her teachings have touched and gives it all to God, recognizing that of themselves these things could not have been done.

I learned, too, to be tempted. When those would come to me who were sick found healing in my presence, it was tempting to want to say, "Yes, look what I've done. I've really earned this. I spent forty days and forty nights in the desert. I've been to India and Tibet. I've been to England. I've studied with all of the masters of Egypt. Yes, I really deserve to be seen as a healer and a teacher."

But I learned through humility to remember the simplicity that of myself, I can do nothing. I cultivated within myself the art of always being a *student* of Love, and not the *professor* of Love, who thinks he is done just because he has a lot of letters after his name.

As you progress, and as you allow more of the abundance of God's Love to flow through you, you begin to stand up out of the crowd, and you begin to attract those that want the light. As that occurs, you must practice discipline and vigilance by remembering humility always, until you are remembering it with every breath.

LESSON 5: *The Keys to the Kingdom*

Why? If you are living in this world, and feel that no one looks up to you, no one takes you as an authority, there is only one reason. You have resisted the truth of your being, and through denial have pushed God's Light away out of your fear, your deep-seated fear, that you might appear to be different than everybody else.

The world would teach you to be a doormat so that you fit in and do not ruffle anybody's feathers. But as you become empowered, one way you will know that it is occurring is that some people will not like you. You will push their buttons just by walking into the room, for darkness abhors light. It is that simple.

Humility is absolutely essential. Through the doorway of humility, the light of power can be turned on through you in ever-greater voltages. If that voltage does not seem to be flowing through your mind, look well to see if you are remembering humility and giving yourself to it.

For the Light of God can only shine through you to the degree that you are willing to take responsibility for it, which involves giving the fruits of it back to its Source, and not claiming it as your own. When you claim *nothing* for yourself, *all* things can flow through you. The Holy Spirit can gather millions of beings to come to you in many planes, because it knows you will not distort the Love of God by usurping God's position and putting yourself upon the throne.

Humility is a chief characteristic to cultivate. Therefore, when you pray, indeed, ask for greatness. Let the Father know that you are ready for the fullness of Christ to be incarnate, and simply hold the promise within that you will always remember that you are not the doer and the maker. You are merely the one who has come to recognize that only the Love of God can fulfill you as a soul. Only the fulfillment of your purpose to be a channel for Love can bring you the success that you truly seek.

When you are fully committed to that, rather than being committed to wondering about other people's opinions, then that power can begin to move through you.

When you are willing to let go of the world, Heaven will come to replace it. When you are willing to let go of your need for egoic grand-

LESSON 5: *The Keys to the Kingdom*

ness, true grandeur will begin to pour forth through you. There is a paradox within Spirit. Learn to discern it. Become a master of it. And never neglect the need for discipline based on the foundation of humility.

You see, this is what has caused you to fear the energy of desire, because in the past (and that can go back a long way), you have decided to find out what it would be like to let all of that power be claimed as your own, to be used to serve the voice of ego. That is what you are afraid of. But if you cultivate these stages and ground them in humility, you will never need to fear the misuse of desire.

Therefore, in your prayers, as often as you can remember to do so, remember that what you decree *is*. So speak clearly within yourself:

> Source, Creator, God, Goddess,
> All That Is, Abba
> I am ready to be what you created me to be.
> I choose to remember that I am effect and not cause.
> Thy will be done, knowing that your will is my full happiness.

> Reveal then, that path through which that happiness can be known.
>
> For my way has never worked, but your way always does.

Then, in each day remember the energy of appreciation. It is well and good to appreciate one another. But in the privacy of your own meditation and prayer, appreciate how the power of that Source of Love I have called God is living and moving and breathing to bring the people, the books, the teachers, and the experiences that are gently unraveling the cocoon of ego around you. And awakening you to the truth, beauty, majesty, grandeur, and greatness that Life Itself *is*.

Life wants to breathe through you as magically and powerfully as it breathes through a thunderstorm, or the leaf on a tree, or the radiance in a newborn baby's eyes.

That Life is what you are. That Life is the presence of God's Love, the depth of the ocean welling up into the waves of creation. Let, therefore, that Life alone be your guide in all things, and rest in appreciation before the infinite mystery that Life is, and say "yes" to it! Say "yes" to

Lesson 5: *The Keys to the Kingdom*

Life—that you are willing to let the fullness of it wash through you and carry you into an ever-deepening understanding and comprehension of all that God is. If you would well receive it, resting in the awareness of divine humility is the sweetest of experiences that you can ever know.

Many of you look upon me and say, "Oh, would I ever love to be where Jeshua is!" Think a thought and you are with someone. Think a thought and you are in that universe.

I tell you this, where I abide is in a vibrational frequency with many, many other beings whose consciousness *never wavers* for an instant from the deep *appreciation* and *humility* before the mystery of all that God is. We abide in the great delight of knowing that we live, yet not us, but our Creator lives *as us*.

The only difference between being a master and being a student is that the master has mastered the art of always being a student. Think about that one.

Desire, intention, allowance, surrender—what do you *truly* want? Are you willing to feel it and let that thread of desire carry you home? Can you remember to use time constructively by focusing your intention, by reminding yourself of what you are truly here for? You are not here to survive; you are here to *live* as the truth of who you are.

Allowance is not a passive acceptance of things as they are, but a recognition that there is something quite beautiful at work. There is an intelligence, a Love that knows you better than you know yourself and is presenting you, moment to moment, with jewels and gems and blessings and lessons that something is weaving the tapestry of your life, and nothing is happening by accident.

Surrender is the cultivation of the recognition that your happiness can be found only in the submission of your will to the will of God. For your will has been to be in conflict and struggle and limitation. God's will is that you live without conflict, in peace, joy, fulfillment and happiness. It is called bliss.

If ever you wonder how to anchor your awareness in humility, stop what you are doing and ask yourself this question:

> Did I create myself?

You know well that the answer is:

LESSON 5: *The Keys to the Kingdom*

No, I don't even know when I was created.

Something birthed me. What is it?

That will bring you to humility rather quickly. Do you know how to give birth to a star? No! Do you know how to give birth to a leaf on a tree? No! Do you even know how you lift your hand from your lap? No! What then, do you know? Nothing! Allow yourself to understand that you do not know anything. In that state of divine ignorance, you will rest in the humility that finally allows your Creator to move through you and reveal to you all things.

Beloved friends, The Way of the Heart is that way which corrects perception and brings right-mindedness, so that you are no longer the maker and the doer and the director. Your opinions will come to mean nothing to you whatsoever. Out of a grand emptiness, you will discover a perfect peace. Life will bear you on its wings. Through you, Life will express, in ever greater dimensionality, the exquisite and infinite Love and power and creativity that is God, until you swear that God is all there is. And there will be no place to find a trace of *you*.

For if enlightenment is the ending of separation,

how can there be a maker and doer? Can the wave direct itself? The ego is the attempt to do so, and it always fails.

Peace then, be with you always. Let peace pervade your being at all times. Know that you are safe in the Love of God that arises from that great Source of mystery and would move through you with every breath you breathe and every word you speak, until you hear only that impetus of guidance that wells up from the depth of your being as a gentle voice that you trust completely. And you will know the freedom that you seek.

You already abide where we are. Trust this. Know this. Rely on this. Explore The Way of the Heart and you will come to know the truth of Love.

Be you therefore at peace beloved friends. Amen.

Lesson 6

Love Heals All Things

Indeed, greetings unto you, beloved and holy friends. *Indeed, greetings unto you beloved and holy friends.* If you understand the meaning of this greeting, if you comprehend the depth of each term used, already you know all there is to know. And you are well prepared to extend the Love of God forever.

"Indeed" means simply that there are no other options. "Greetings unto you" means salutations to that One created of the Father before all things, for I bow down before your radiance. "Beloved" and holy Child of God! Indeed, beloved of God. Indeed, beloved of every molecule in your physical universe. Indeed, loved of your Holy Mother, this precious Earth. Indeed, loved by anything you can imagine that has ever existed or ever could exist that has extended itself from the Heart and Mind of God. You are the beloved, pure and simple. And again, there are no options.

"Holy" because you are whole. Not because you have earned that holiness, but because it is that which is the Truth from which you are extended forth forever. Because you are made in the image of God, because you spring forth from the Mind of God, you are holiness itself each time you set aside the temptation to dream a useless dream, and walk this Earth as Christ.

Beloved and holy "friend"—a friend is not one lesser than myself. A friend is one who walks in perfect equality with the grandest of masters, whomever you might conceive such a master to be. A friend is one who chooses to look upon another and see only the face of Christ therein. There is no one who shall receive these words who has not already looked upon *me* and seen the face of Christ within. And likewise, I look upon *you* and call you "friend."

For when I look upon you, I see not the very momentary dreams that you seem to think are lasting so long. I see only the radiance of that which the Father has extended out of Love. I see only that which has neither beginning nor ending. I see only that which knows neither birth nor death. I see only that which has no limitations. I see only

LESSON 6: *Love Heals All Things*

that—the light of which is already extended throughout all dimensions and all universes.

I see only my brother and my sister. And I see not a trace of inequality between us. Yet I do recognize that, within your dream, it appears to you that I have gone ahead just a little bit.

At times, within your hearts, there is a longing to follow me. If you would but heed that longing, if you would make that longing primary at all times, your own desire will bring you wholly to where I am. And you will laugh when you discover that you have not moved an inch—that where I am is where you are, and where you are is in eternity, not in time; that where you are is in the place of your birth: the Mind of God.

This is the only thing that is true and it is true always. This is the only reality that you genuinely possess. Therefore, indeed, I call you *friend*. For well do I see that you are as I am. Therefore, indeed, greetings unto you, beloved and holy friends.

There is nothing else to be said. Yet the mind races, does it not? It races away from the very reality that I have just described about you. The mind races from that Source as a sunbeam from the sun. Yet in reality, it never leaves its Source. The very power with which you seem to become distracted by a momentary thought of fear is the same power by which you will awaken to your own call.

If You Would Know Love, Know Your Self

In truth, there is a place within you that already knows the day and the hour. You already know when you are going to decide to live the decision to be awake in God, to be only the presence of Love. Love embraces all things, allows all things, trusts all things, and thereby, transcends all things. Love is never possessive. Love is never fearful. Love is simply Love. Love cannot shine with specialness upon anyone at any time. For specialness, itself, is a contraction; the attempt to take Love and make it shine only on one object, only on one person, only on one being, only within one universe.

Therefore, whenever you recognize that you have singled someone or something out and said, "They hold a greater value," you may rest assured that you are not in Love at all. You are in

LESSON 6: *Love Heals All Things*

fear. And if that one were to leave you, where would you be? But if you are *in Love* as a fish within the sea, all beings can arise and pass away and you will bless them in their journey. You will remember that you reside where God has placed you: in Her Heart. When you choose to be *only* the presence of Love, even the dream of loss will dissolve from your consciousness as a forest mist before the rising sun.

Indeed, beloved friends, Love does wait upon your welcome. Yet you cannot welcome Love by waiting for it to be brought *to* you by another, not even by me. You cannot welcome Love by trying to scurry about to create the environment in which you believe your preferences are being met. You cannot welcome Love when that welcome is attached or linked to any phenomenal thing, anything that has been birthed in time. Love can only be welcomed where Love truly resides. And Love resides within you as the core and the Source of your very being.

Therefore, if you would know Love, know your Self. Embrace the truth about it and the Truth will set you free. Then, indeed, Love will flow *through* you. Like the great sunlight that comes to nurture this beloved Earth, the Love that flows through you will be unimpeded. It will not meet an obstacle. You will look upon whomever is in front of you and you will know that they are sent unto you of the Father. The Holy Spirit has guided them to you because, through you, Love can be given in a way that begins to touch the place of their awakening. That is why you are but the servant of Love. That is all that life is!

When you choose to surrender, to give up the game, to give up the dream of trying to resist the Truth that is true about you always, you will become a mere channel, a mere conduit. You will become no more a seeker, for you will have decided to have *found*. When you have surrendered the last vestige of an insane possibility of contracting away from the Truth, when you have given that up, Love will flow through you. But notice that if it flows *through* you, it must first flow *to* you. Therefore, seek always to receive in order to give. For what can you give another if you have not yet received it to yourself?

How many of you have been taught to *try* to love, to *try* to do the "right" thing, the "good" thing? Yet, how many times have you gone within

LESSON 6: *Love Heals All Things*

your secret chamber and said, "I am unworthy"? Then you wonder why your attempts to join in love with others never seem to be quite fulfilling enough, never quite seem to fill the cup, never quite seem to elicit the joy that you believe could be there.

Listen well: your work—if you wish to call it that—is not to seek and find love. It is merely to turn within to discover every obstacle that you have created to its presence, and to offer that obstacle to the great dissolver of dreams, the grace of the Holy Spirit.

I have said unto you many times that the greatest of gifts you can give is this: to come wholly to the recognition that every attempt you have made to resist being the presence of Christ has failed you miserably. No matter how many times you have tried to convince yourself that you are unworthy, yet does the universe find a way to Love you. No matter how many times you have tried to lock yourself into the space and volume of a body, it has not succeeded. And at death, you have remembered and been confronted with the radiance of your unlimitedness.

Therefore, the greatest of gifts you can give another is to be one who has rescinded the need to insist on the insanity of fear.

The Primary Characteristic of Mastery

Fearlessness is the primary characteristic of mastery. Mastery is not having great power to make things happen. It is only the recognition that what is true is true always and there *is* no other choice. Free will does not mean that you have the right to believe that you can succeed at being other than what God created you to be. Having free will does not mean that you can elect not to take the only curriculum that life is offering to you in every moment. It means only that you *do* have the right to put it off yet another day. And each time you put it off, you slumber in your suffering.

But when you elect to take the only curriculum that matters, when you elect to use the power of your free will to say:

> Now, from this moment on, I will no longer tolerate error in myself.
>
> No more games, no more dreams. I am

LESSON 6: *Love Heals All Things*

committed to being only the presence of
Love, for that is the Truth of who I am.

It matters not the opinions of others who are yet resisting that decision. Then, indeed, all things under Heaven and Earth move to support you, to guide you to the right person, the right place, the right book, the right sunrise, the right meadow in order to assist you in dropping the shackles of the obstacles to the presence of Love that you have created as an idol and as a substitute for Love.

That is why when you truly pray from the depth of your soul, "God, bring me home," you may rest assured, from that moment on it is fine to trust every little thing that unfolds. For though you see it not, what you call angels—friends that simply do not have bodies—are rushing about because you have given the command:

> Yes, I accept your presence in my life.
> I turn the whole thing over.
> Now, each moment is dedicated to healing
> and awakening the illusory sense of separation from God that once I created in error.

In how many ways have you sought Love? Can you count the ways? Would you dare to try to count each little pebble of sand on the beaches of your planet? Each and every soul has already tried to seek out Love in that many ways—if not more. You have sought it in a million forms in which you already knew that you could not find it. All because you wanted to perpetuate the insane attempt to try to separate yourself from God. And that is as futile as a sunbeam trying to separate itself from the sun.

Indeed, beloved friends, there is only one question you need answer:

What am I choosing in this moment?

What have I given mastery over my life unto? What perception, what thought, what feeling? Feeling merely flows from the thought or the perception you have chosen. What behavior, what action am I choosing in this moment and does it express the reality of my being? Am I being busy extending love, or am I busying myself fearfully trying to grasp at what I *think* can give me love so that I do not lose it?

Look well, then, upon your parents, your siblings, your mates, and your friends. Not one of them—*not one of them*—holds the power to

LESSON 6: *Love Heals All Things*

bring love to you. So what are you trying to get from them? Why do you ever insist that another ought to be conformed to what you believe you need? It is futile—one hundred percent, absolutely, positively futile—to *seek* love in relationship with anything or anyone.

It is, however, quite appropriate to *extend* Love in each relationship, with everyone and everything. But the extension of that Love requires that you have awakened to the truth that the *only* relationship that truly holds value is the relationship between you as the soul and God as your Creator.

Imagine a light bulb in one of your fixtures, that looks out from its little filaments and says, "Well I hope the person that just walked in the door is the right one. If I could just reach out and grab them, maybe my own light would come on."

Is it not a lot easier to simply take the cord and plug it into the right socket? How many times are you going to insist on trying to plug your cord into the wrong socket? "Well that one didn't work. I'll try this body; I'll try this person. I'll try this career. Not getting very much juice from that either." And then you get angry because it is not giving you enough juice, or it gave you enough juice yesterday, but not today, so it must be *its* fault.

There is one little tiny socket into which you can plug your cord. It is the only one that it fits in and it is the only socket wired to bring you the flowing and living waters of grace. That socket dwells only within your heart. Not the physical heart, but that which is symbolized by the physical heart: the core of your very being. But how many times in each day do you check to see that the cord is still plugged in? How many times do you remember to ask yourself:

> Is my commitment to Love or
> is my commitment to fear?

Fear is the act of disconnecting your cord from the only socket that can truly satisfy you, and running about trying to plug it in to somebody else's or something else's. I would ask you to consider this one question, as you look upon the whole of your experience: Has it ever worked? Can it ever work?

Imagine trying to hold flowing water in the palm of your hand by squeezing the fingers together. How much are you left with? Does it not just run through the fingers, no matter how hard you try?

Lesson 6: *Love Heals All Things*

It finds the little holes and it flows away. You open your hand and there is not enough left there to wet the tongue.

Yet, each time you have looked upon another—whether parent or sibling or friend or mate or teacher or whatever physical person or object—and tried to plug into that socket to get the juice you believe you need, that is just what you are doing. And you literally end up squeezing the life out of the relationship itself.

When you seek first the Kingdom and plug that cord into the socket within your heart, when you remember that you and your Father are one, that only Love is real, and nothing else matters, you will remember that the temptation to find Love outside your Self is nothing more than the echo of an old habit. And that habit cannot live unless *you* feed it.

Therefore, feed the only habit that matters: the habit of remembering that the Truth is true always, regardless of what is passing before your physical eyes and before your mind. In all comings and goings, in all births and deaths, in all arising and passing away of universe after universe after universe, in the midst of a flat tire or a sudden rainstorm, nothing—*nothing*—holds value except your relationship with your Creator.

When you have experienced in relationship with anyone or anything a moment of bliss, a moment of a peace that forever passes all understanding, a moment of fulfillment so sweet and so sublime that no word could touch it, much less express it, what you have experienced is only the flow of the Love of God *through* you. That person or thing did not cause it. It was caused because, for just a moment, you stepped out of your drama, you stepped out of your dream, and allowed the Truth to be lived.

Then, of course, you tricked yourself into believing, "God, that was so sweet! That was the best thing I've ever tasted. It must have come from *you*. Get over here! I *need* you!" If ever you believe you need anything or anyone, rest assured, in that moment you are living in delusion.

All You Need Is Love

All you need is Love. Love fulfills all things. Love embraces all things. Love heals all things. Love transforms all things. Therefore, remember well: you, and only you, can become the cause of

Lesson 6: *Love Heals All Things*

your fulfillment, your peace, and your completion of time. This requires that you do nothing save remember to establish the connection with your Creator.

Is it not true that what you desire most of all is Love? Is it not true that you hope that each relationship—no matter how short, no matter what its form—that each journey, that each undertaking will allow you the experience of peace? Is it not true that you, who find yourselves in and as a body temporarily in time, is it not true that the grandest of experiences you have known have been those that seem to flood the very cells of the body with Love, with a sublime bliss and a peace? Accept that truth, that what you desire beyond all things is the living experience of Love.

Then remember this:

> Nothing you do can bring Love to you.
> Nothing you do can keep Love for yourself in a form of your choosing.
> Nothing you do—nothing you do—can make Love appear in the form of your insistence.

Release the drama, release the dream, and choose to remember the truth that is true always. Return to the Kingdom within, even prior to every breath. Remind yourself and say to your Creator:

> I want only that which is true always.
> Love is what I want. Love is what you are.
> Love is what I receive. Love is who I am.
> I and my Father are one.

Here and here alone do you discover what you seek. Then, you become free to walk this Earth, to be in the world, but not of it at all. And though your friends will look upon you and still see a man or a woman who seems to act much like them, yet though they see it not, Christ dwells with them. Something in them keeps attracting them to you. They are not sure what it is. Is it the shape of your body or the radiance of your eyes? It is not these things. They feel the quality of *Love*.

Can you imagine walking upon this Earth and no matter where you are, feeling as though every wisp of cloud and every blade of grass and all good things under Heaven and Earth were already residing with you, within this sphere of your countenance? Can you imagine walking upon this Earth and sensing that the light from the farthest of stars that shines during the night is already within you, that the whole of creation was held in the palms of your hands? Would there be room yet to convince yourself that there is something you lack, something you need, that the restlessness you feel must be valid?

In truth, you are like one who has been given a perfect treasure, a priceless jewel. You have placed it into your pocket and forgotten that you possess it. So you run around trying to look into everybody else's pocket. You have tried to seduce certain ones to surrender so that you can own the clothing and, therefore, try to possess the jewel that you hope is in their pocket. But the great truth is that you cannot possess Love until you set it free. You cannot move into holy relationship with anyone or anything until you give up all trace of need to possess it.

When your only desire is Love, you will be willing to set anyone free, to support him or her in their own journey, no matter what it is or what it takes. Yet, you will never feel your Love waver.

If a twinge of sadness arises because you recognize that two bodies in space are now going to go to separate parts of the planet, as that twinge arises, you will recognize it as the effect of a mistaken perception. You will move within, to the place in which all minds are joined. You will remember that your fulfillment does not rest in *gaining* love from another, but in *giving* Love to everyone.

If, indeed, you would know the Truth that sets you free, heed each and every word that is being shared. If you would taste the sweet nectar of perfect freedom, be committed to replacing every erroneous perception you have ever made and every thought you have ever held of everyone and everything. Set these things aside and commit the fullness of your energy to the simple, but vigilant practice of remembering the Truth—even prior to every breath:

> I live!—yet not I—but Christ dwells in me. Therefore, I submit and surrender to the Truth that is true always. My fulfillment comes only from allowing Christ to be given to the world.

The Truth is very simple. It is not complex at all. Get out of the way, and let Love live through you. And all of a sudden you will know that, indeed, you are given all good things eternally. You will

Lesson 6: *Love Heals All Things*

know that grace is reality. You will know that effortlessness is the way of life in the Kingdom.

But effortlessness does not mean that you do not feel, for you are in a dimension of feeling. Effortlessness does not mean that you do not discover how to deepen your ability to be the living embodiment of Love. It does not mean that you do not challenge yourself to learn to express Love in a way that can be heard by another. Effortlessness means simply that you abandon the resistance to what Love requires in each moment.

Effortlessness is the way of the Kingdom. In the world, effortlessness means that you let down the wall you have built between yourself and all of creation. You no longer resist *the lived experience of relationship,* whatever it is—relationship with a cloud, relationship with another person, relationship with a dog or a cat, relationship with April 15th when you write your government a check. Why not wrap it with Christmas paper and ribbons and send it with much Love?

When you have learned to release the barriers or the walls between yourself and whatever is in front of you, when you open the door to your chakras—the body's energy centers—and simply allow Love to be lived through you, when you look upon another person or another situation or another thing and realize that nothing in this world has the power to hurt you and nothing in this world has the power to take anything from you, you are free. If you remember to extend Love, then you are free! You have transcended birth and death. The seeker is no more and only Christ walks this Earth.

Feeling Is the Doorway to Love and Freedom

If your commitment is, indeed, to look within and discover each and every obstacle you have ever created to the presence of Love, why do you resist *feeling* those things? For well has it been said to you, that on just the other side is the very Love you seek.

Deny not the role of *feeling* in this dimension, for feeling is everything! You cannot even know the presence of God unless you feel it. You cannot *think about* the presence of God. You cannot insist on a belief about the presence of God. That does not do it; that does not fill your cup. Feeling fills

Lesson 6: *Love Heals All Things*

your cup. Feeling—unbridled, unblocked, unobstructed feeling—is the doorway to that Love that sets you free!

Therefore, when you say, "I don't want to feel this," rest assured you are truly saying, "Yes, the doorway to the Kingdom of Heaven is right in front of me, but if you think I'm going to open it, you are crazy! It's not worth it anyway. What is worth it is protecting the substitute I have made."

I have called this the ego, the false self, what I once described to you as a gnat shouting at space, "That's what I'm committed to. And I'm going to protect this thing. Give up Heaven to protect this useless little thing? Oh, yes! You'd better believe I'd be willing to make that sacrifice! What's Heaven anyway? A bunch of love stuff, a bunch of people running around in bliss, some of them without bodies, hanging out in unlimitedness, fearlessness, and utter fulfillment. Who needs it? Oh, but this little gnat, this little gnat of mine. Oh! I'm going to make it shine!"

How many times have you tried to make that little gnat shine? For instance, "Everybody notice, it's shining. Please, notice how great I am. I'm making my gnat shine. Listen to my whining and my complaining, and the lamenting, the great sadness. Oh! How grand my gnat is!"

Meanwhile, the Love of God flows through a multitude of universes and creates—forever—even new universes. And the Love of God does not even notice the gnat at all. No one is paying any attention. Your friends around you do not want to pay attention, although sometimes you corner them and they have no choice. But those of us without bodies, do you really actually think we waste our precious eternity taking your attempt to make the gnat shine seriously? Indeed, because we Love you, we give you the space, and we honor your free will to be as little and as miserable as you wish.

We will wait until you choose to come once again into the greatness in which you truly reside. We never withdraw our Love from you. We simply look through your story line because what *we* wish to Love is the Christ that dwells within you.

What day and hour will you decide to love yourself as God has first Loved you? To truly —to *truly*— once and for all, make the decision to *live*! For until

Lesson 6: *Love Heals All Things*

you decide to live *with*, and *for*, and forever *from* the Mind of Christ, life has not yet begun!

Right away the mind reacts, "Oh, my God! That's a bit of a blow, isn't it? Look at all the experiences I've had, Jeshua. How can you tell me I haven't lived? Why, there was this drama, then there was that drama, then there was that drama over there. Don't you remember seventeen lifetimes ago when I did this and then I did that? I struggled through that one, and I've struggled through this one. I have lived."

No, you have *dreamed*.

Do you awaken in the morning and realize that you have had a whole night of dreams of receiving ribbons and trophies, and what have you, from the world? And then say, "That was very real. The trophies must be out sitting on my kitchen table." While you dreamt, it felt real enough. And that is the quality I am speaking to here. If you wish to take this as an affront, it is perfectly fine. It will not disturb my peace at all.

Until you fully decide to come into life as the presence of Christ, as the presence of Love, and to *own* each moment of your experience as wholly self-created, for no other reason than that you have chosen it from the perfect and infinite freedom of your unlimited being, life has not yet begun. When you look upon all things without judgment through the eyes of forgiveness, when you decide to embody only the reality of Love no matter what anybody else is doing, that is when life begins!

As of this date on your calendar, there have only been a handful of beings who have *truly lived life* upon this plane, a very small handful. There are many of us that would just absolutely be thrilled if *you* would join the club!

I will let you in on a little secret: until you do, you do not get to graduate. You will never leave this plane, filled with conflict and suffering, as it seems to be, until you have lived the experience of walking this Earth wholly as the thought of Love in form, with no other allegiances, but to Love. You will never leave this plane. You will never take up your cross and follow me. You will spin around again and again and again, only to be confronted by the same need to decide wholly for Love.

Lesson 6: *Love Heals All Things*

You will finally look heavenward and say, "Father, let's get on with it. Enough time has been wasted. It's gone, its fine, it doesn't matter. *Now*! I am committed to Love. Bring on whatever I *must* experience to bring up from the depth—the places where I've hidden it within me—every obstacle that must yet be dissolved by the light of the grace of perfect Love.

"And I will do whatever I can, from my side of the fence, to open up those places, to feel those places, to embrace those places, to love those places, to claim those places as wholly self-created. I will let my parents off the hook. I will let my siblings off the hook. I will let my great, great, great, great, great, great grandfather off the hook. I will let Adam and Eve off the hook. I will let the government off the hook. And I will love myself enough to heal my separation from God.

"I will be humble enough to recognize that if I'm having an experience—because I know I have made the commitment to healing—then you have indeed, precious Father, brought me all good things. For this moment of experience can be seen through eyes that recognize that it is but a stepping stone to the perfect peace that I seek.

"My life is no longer mine, for I know not how to correct that one fundamental error. But I *can* surrender into feeling each moment fully while choosing Love anyway. And Love will dissolve the pain that I have carried all because I insisted on trying to separate myself from the Source of my being. This little gnat of mine is being put to rest. For the only thing that can shine is Christ."

For Christ—the sons and daughters of God, the offspring of God—is God's only creation. The rest of it is attributed to *you*. Even space and time is yours. Your Creator's only creation is *you*, the truth of you. For you are Love, and God creates only that which is like unto Himself. And God is *only* Love.

Many of you believe you are on a spiritual path. You will know if that is true by your willingness to feel and experience wholly exactly what is in front of you, moment to moment. So if you have a conflict with another and you sit in your chair and decide to pray or meditate in order to change

Lesson 6: *Love Heals All Things*

the feeling state within yourself, and you arise later and say, "There, I'm feeling much better now," but the issue has not been solved with another, *nothing has changed*.

Go, therefore, to the other. Open your heart, share, and resolve. If you have offended another, ask them their forgiveness. If you have judged another, admit it. Ask for their forgiveness. It is only in such a way that you can truly heal the place of conflict within.

Beloved friends, the essence of this lesson is quite simple: Where are you *now*? Are you willing to allow yourself to see everything around you and within you as the doorway to the Kingdom of Heaven, waiting only for you to acknowledge its presence and to open it? Are you willing to truly be right where you are—*wholly, right where you are*? And the mind says, "Well, of course. I'm on a spiritual path." Rest assured, if you look well into your feelings and find any trace of resistance, you have not yet made the necessary commitment that gives you the *power* to open that door.

Only Through Feeling Do You Awaken

Feeling is the message of this lesson. For it is only through feeling that you truly awaken. Concepts and ideas can begin to direct the mind to believe that there is something out there that is attractive that might even be better than what you have been doing before. But concepts and ideas do not, in themselves, open the door. They are symbols, and that is all. A symbol cannot quench your thirst. It is only at the level of genuine *feeling* that you can once again know the presence of God who dwells within you, around you and through you, even now.

Feel what you have created as a substitute for the truth. Own it, look upon it, and then let it go. Learn that regardless of what choice you may have made in the past, once you have embraced it, once you have felt it, you remain perfectly innocent and imbued with the power to choose again to *feel*, to learn once again to *feel* the glorious warmth that permeates the Kingdom of Heaven.

Nothing you do with time can match the importance of what we have shared in this lesson. Nothing you do in the field of time holds a candle

Lesson 6: *Love Heals All Things*

to the incredible gift that is waiting for you. Therefore, use time constructively by deciding to love, that Love may teach you of itself. Indeed, beloved and holy friends, when you have done this, you will find yourself translated into a form that could never possibly be contained by the space and volume of a physical body.

You will look upon this entire dimension as a mere temporary learning device. You will set it aside, as a child sets aside a toy that has been outgrown. But you will do it with deep appreciation and love for the toy that you have played with for so long. You will carry with you a deep sense of gratitude for everything this physical dimension has brought to you.

There will be not a molecule of beingness within you that will feel any resentment, any longing, any anger, or any remorse for anything. All of your experience will have become wholly acceptable to you. For it was by such experience that you were finally driven to want only the Truth.

From this day forward you will never again be able to truly convince yourself that all of your attempts to stay distracted or conformed to the world are really accomplishing a thing. You will find that your mind begins to penetrate the unconscious habits you have created in an attempt to hide from what must yet be felt. You will know perfectly well when you are simply deluding yourself. You will start to smile and say, "Oh, yes, there I go again. Might as well set that aside. And plant my feet firmly on the ground and, indeed, live with passion from the Truth of the Kingdom of Heaven!"

In The Way of the Heart, we will speak ever more directly and even more forcefully to you. For the time comes quickly when this planet will not be willing to tolerate untidy house guests that are not willing to vibrate at the frequency of being toward which the planet herself is preparing to move. Therefore, be not caught by coming home one day and discovering that the landlord has changed the locks and you have not a place to rest your head.

Rather, become the living embodiment of Love and journey with your Holy Mother into an entirely new dimension of being. And never forget to sing, laugh, dance and play along the way!

Be you therefore, at peace beloved friends. Amen.

LESSON 7

BIRTHING THE MIND OF CHRIST

Forever, I am with you. *Forever, I am with you.* For long before the stars were birthed, long before the planets arose, long before even a thought of physicality had emerged within the divine mind of the Son of God, we were already created together and equally. Yet, that creation of what alone is real knows no point of birth.

Therefore, because the Father is forever, so too, have we abided together and been sustained together in Love. Throughout all time and even unto eternity do we abide together in the Reality of who we are. Therefore, think it not extraordinary when I say unto you: I am with you always, even unto the end of this age.

What journey have *you* ever taken that is not familiar to *me*? What journey have I ever taken that is, in truth, not familiar to you? For when you look upon me from some deep place of knowingness within, though the words may be different, you say within yourself, "Behold! Christ appears before me."

When you hold a thought of me in the mind and the body is flooded with emotion, soft and gentle and light, and you recognize that the holy Son of God was birthed and perfected in your friend, Jeshua ben Joseph, what is it within you that *knows* that this is the truth? What part of your mind, what capacity within your heart can look upon me and recognize the Truth within me, so that you love me? For I say well unto you, it is the same as that part of *my* mind, that part of *my* heart that looks upon you and says, "Behold! The holy Child of God is before me. And I Love this one."

That which *knows*, that which comprehends immediately is the Mind of Christ. It recognizes itself in each and every one. That Mind of Christ dwells within you in its fullness *now*! Therefore, as I have said unto you many times, never fail to remember that it takes one to know one. If you would look upon me and say, "Beloved friend, thank you," look well upon yourself and say, "Beloved friend, thank you." Allow the breath to flow.

LESSON 7: *Birthing the Mind of Christ*

How many journeys have there been? How many moments of experience passed under the bridge of your beingness before you first began to re-awaken to the Truth that is true always? How many lifetimes, how many worlds, before a light began to dawn, so imperceptibly at first that it was not recognized? And a tiny voice whispered from a place that seemed so far removed from where you dwelt:

> Beloved son, you are with me now.
>
> You remain as I have created you to be.
>
> Therefore, be at peace. You are loved.

The voice seemed so far away, so faint, that surely, it could not be your own. Surely, it was just a moment's fantasy.

In the midst of some journey, you paused. And as a raindrop fell upon a leaf and your eyes looked upon that experience, you felt and knew that you were *one* with the leaf and the raindrop, and that, indeed, you *were* those things. How many moments of experience passed by before these kinds of qualities began to emerge in your consciousness, as what seemed at first to be tiny mad ideas? Thoughts such as, "My God, I just felt myself to be one with all of creation. Well, better not tell anyone about that!" And off you went.

But the moments began to come more often, still perhaps fleetingly, and yet now more familiar—a sense underneath all of the drama, all of the crying, all of the lamenting, all of the resenting, all of the fearing, all of the striving, and all of the seeking. The still tiny voice would come and say:

> Beloved son, you remain as I have created you to be.
> You are loved.
> You are wholly loving and wholly lovable forever.

The tiny voice would still steal through the roar and the din that had seemed to make a home within your mind. Rest assured, you would not be where you appear to be in this moment, if you had not already begun to experience many moments that express the quality that I have just described to you, of truly hearing the still, small voice of the Comforter within.

Therefore, indeed, each of you knows that there is a longing within you that *cannot* and *will not* any longer be denied. You *know* from the Christ

Lesson 7: Birthing the Mind of Christ

within you that Christ has stirred within you, and is rising to take up its rightful place as the master of your mind and your heart, your body and your breath, and your dreams and your passions! Each of you knows that it is absolutely futile to attempt to settle for anything less.

It does not come because of anything I have ever done *for* you. It comes because it *must* come. It must arise within each created mind regardless of its journeys, regardless of its attempts to deny what is eternally true. That is called the illusion of the dream of separation. It must come and it is inevitable because Christ *will not* be denied. Christ *cannot* be denied because only Christ can express what is absolutely true.

Only Christ can so *inform* the cellular structure of the body that even the simplest of gestures extends Love unto another who beholds it. Only Christ knows how to breathe the breath that releases all trauma, all hurt. Only Christ understands the power of true forgiveness, which is always, by the way, forgiveness of one's self, since no one has wronged you at any time.

Only Christ can bring a smile to the lips of a

body, such that when another looks upon you and sees that smile, their heart is filled. Only Christ can walk in this world, yet not be of the world. And only Christ can transcend every limited and fearful creation, transforming them into the beautiful flower that blossoms and gives its sweet fragrance to all of creation. Is it not that which you long to feel moving through your being? Is not that call to awaken alive within you? Oh, beloved friends, you know that it is!

Love you, therefore, one another. And love you, therefore, the Self that has been given unto you of the Father. Learn to hear *only* that voice. Learn to desire *only* that voice. Learn to follow only that voice that knows the Truth is true always:

> I and my heavenly Father are one.
> This world is but a passing shimmer
> and a dream.
> It holds no value save that which
> Christ can bring to it.
> Only Love is real.
> Anything else is the choice to momentarily
> believe in illusion.

Rest assured, illusion within an illusory world

Lesson 7: Birthing the Mind of Christ

can seem to hold great power. But all power has been given unto you. All power under Heaven and Earth is given unto the holy Child of God. And that power dwells within you as the Life of your life, the breath of your breath, the Truth of your truth, the being of your being, and the joy of your joy. There has never been an illusory creation that has ever, in truth, threatened it. Nor can any illusion take reality from you.

The only thing that can occur is that you use that power to believe in loss. All forms of loss that you perceive through the physical eyes or through the worldly mind are nothing more than passing shades of your insistence on believing that loss is possible. All forms of the contraction known as fear are nothing more than temporary modifications of the very power given unto you—a power that you have sought to use to see if it were possible to convince yourself that something besides Love is real.

But the story is over. The dream of separation is ending. The whole of creation is now experiencing a growing power, a movement, and a momentum that must carry the mind, from which creation springs, to a new level. It is not so much an evolutionary level as a level of re-cognition, a level of re-membrance, a level of re-turning.

That wave of momentum is alive and has already arisen within your heart and mind. You know it. Stop denying it. Stop questioning it. Stop looking for signs from the world around you that it is all right to feel it.

Accept it as a divine gift from your Creator. For the call has gone out. Though many listen, few hear, and fewer still become wholly devoted to responding. Therefore, let your prayer be always:

> May Christ, alone, dwell within and as this creation that I once thought was myself.
>
> May Christ, alone, inform each thought and each breath and each choice.
>
> May Love direct each step. May Love transform this journey through time, that in time, I might truly know the reality of eternity, the sanctity of peace, the holiness—the holiness—of intimacy, and the joy of the Father's Love, prior to every breath and, indeed, even prior to every thought that arises within the mind.

Lesson 7: *Birthing the Mind of Christ*

For when you know that you are holiness itself, how could you ever look upon your brother or sister and believe that they have wronged you? How could you ever want to do anything but love them? That is, let the Love of Christ flow through you so deeply and so profoundly that they get that you do not believe their illusion.

When you give unto another that which alone is true, because all minds are joined, you have offered unto them the only gift that holds value. When you give another the truth—perhaps even without saying a word—because all minds are joined they recognize what has been offered and say to themselves, "The one before me knows the truth of me and is looking right through every one of my attempts to be less than who I am. Therefore, I see that it's safe to choose again." That is when miracles occur.

Do not strive to heal this world. Do not do anything to make a show of how much you love another. Give up the concept of being a busy bee. Simply *be* the presence of Love, because you *know* that there is absolutely no value in being anything else. And that, in truth, you have never succeeded at being anything but the presence of Love.

Each sane moment that you have experienced, each moment of unlimitedness, each moment of genuine intimacy, each moment of grace-filled joy that you have ever known, in whatever form it seems to appear, has come because you have allowed your mind to slip into the sea of peace. There you have merely abided, empty, wanting nothing, seeking nothing, being merely the presence of what you are.

When that quality becomes cultivated so that it permeates your consciousness with each breath and with each moment, you will know that Christ has, indeed, arisen this day. And you will celebrate Easter with each breath.

The Shadow of Fear

What, then, could ever possibly arise to obstruct the Truth that is true always?

There is an ancient forest on your planet. A forest so high in a rugged mountain valley and so rugged that no one has ever been there. Unknown to the minds of humanity, life goes on in the forest. Deep within the heart of this forest, this morning a little tiny blade of grass seemed to be tossed by an unseen wind. As it was tossed for

Lesson 7: *Birthing the Mind of Christ*

just a fragment of a moment, so subtle and soft was this wind that as the sunlight played against this blade of grass, it cast the smallest of conceivable shadows on a stone just a little bit away from the blade of grass.

No one noticed. The shadow had no effect. The rock did not even notice. No one on the planet noticed. No one in any of the heavens noticed, except me. I needed something to build a story around. That tiny shadow, cast by a little blade of grass momentarily wiggling in a wind in some remote forest, has virtually no effect on the turning of the planets, the creation of new suns, and certainly not one trace of effect on how deeply the Father loves you.

That little shadow is what you have given power to. It *seems* to be able to obstruct the Truth within you from being lived. For the moment, you gave that little tiny shadow power. In that very moment, fear was born. Fear is always a contraction away from Love. And fear makes you smaller than the blade of grass that momentarily seems to cast a shadow and, therefore, obstructs your recognition of the warmth of the sun that bathes you *always*.

The Way of the Heart

When you resist healing, when you struggle to learn to "speak your truth," you may rest assured that something has occurred just prior to that. What is it? It is your decision to believe that the shadow is all-powerful. And that if you heal, if you grow, if you change, if you let Christ live in you, that the little blade of grass and the little tiny shadow it creates for a very temporary moment will come and punish you and crush you.

If you can truly take this story into your being and recognize the utter laughability of such a belief, you will never again *fear* fear. You will never again allow fear to master you and direct the course of your life.

You will learn what it means to trust what is birthed in the heart. And you will arise and you will go forth without fear—with no story at all. You will accomplish whatever creativity wishes to express through you. And the whole while you will know that of yourself you do nothing, but the Father, through you, can do *anything*.

Therefore, what forms of the shadow of that blade of grass are you allowing to run and own and possess your soul?

There are many forms of that shadow, are there

Lesson 7: Birthing the Mind of Christ

not? There are peers and parents and siblings to please. There are governments to bow down before. There are mates and children that must come first. There are bills to pay. There are desires to check and keep in order. There are activities and statements and behaviors—done by others—that require at least seven or eight hours a day for you to analyze and judge them to death and you think, "My, this world is exhausting. But somebody has to do it."

And you thought it was Love that makes the world go around? Trust me, Love does not spin and get nowhere!

Love created you. Love birthed within you as an individual—at least within the dance of time and space—the power to choose, the power to feel, the power to channel light and Love, the power to know that something exists within and as you. That is what Love has done! Has fear ever created anything remotely like that?

So what do you want? Creation or mimicry? Peace or the ability to simply drug yourself with triviality? ✓ Imagine...all power under Heaven and Earth flowing through you with every breath so that your consciousness witnesses, not what you do as the maker or doer, but that which the divine is doing through you in each moment. And you get to marvel at the creativity of Love, the very same Love that moves the sun and the moon and the stars. Now *that* is a delightful pastime!

By the way, you have called the body *your* body, as if you have some right to possess it. Give the body to God. God knows how to use it; you do not. When your life is given to being *only* the presence of Love for no other reason than that you want it to *be*, you will know—because you will be—the Truth that sets all things free:

> The whole of creation is waiting to move through me, and I want to be aware of it. I want my experience, my lived consciousness, to be blissfully absorbed in observing the flow of Love through me.

And if there are any cobwebs in the way of that, you will sweep them out of the way.

When you are in that quality of being, Heaven and Earth will move to become your servant, and not until then. After all, send a conflicted message and nobody shows up for the dance. So now you know what the shadow is. Perhaps sometimes you enjoy dancing with it. But here is the great question:

> Are you going to let the shadow lead or are *you* going to lead?

Birthing the Christ Mind

When your life becomes liberated in that—I am not speaking of perfection as you would know it—when your life becomes *that* motivation, that attitude, that declaration, and that devotion, then perfection will be witnessed through you. For the true meaning of perfection is miracle mindedness where that which saves time occurs. When your life becomes that, when you no longer have any conflicted commitment in your beingness, you will know exactly what the result of my life was for me, because you will *be* that.

Yes, I know that you are worrying, "Does that mean that when I get really close, I'm going to have to go through my final initiation of crucifixion? And if I have to do it, will you promise that they at least sterilize the nails? Could I choose the day or the hour? I don't like to get up too early."

You already know what crucifixion is all about. You have done it to yourself a million times in ways far worse than a mere nail driven through the hand that creates a little twinge of pain. Hell is nothing more than the state of being rutted, or stuck, in the process of crucifying one's Self, which is the attempt to murder and destroy what God has created out of Love.

Stop wasting your energy *trying* to love God. That will not do it for you. Stop wasting so much energy *trying* to learn how to love another. That will not do it for you. And for *God's* sake, please refrain from all attempts to get anyone to believe that you love them!

Put the whole of your attention on giving up the patterns of belief from which you have attempted to crucify the Self that God made and placed within you as your very *awareness* of your existence. Learn to love that Self beyond all created things. Learn to nurture that Self. Learn to cultivate within that Self only that which speaks of joy and truth. So that your words and your actions and your very presence always uplift another. So that when another walks into the room in which you are sitting or standing or

Lesson 7: *Birthing the Mind of Christ*

moving, they feel like a breath of fresh air just hit them, even if you have not lifted a finger.

As long as there is a trace of energy within you in which you are striving to get from any perceived thing or object around you what you are sure you lack inside yourself, you cannot know the love of Self. And you cannot experience freedom. Happiness is an inside job.

Then, what happens? You finally get it right and you decide, "All right, what's that little shadow been doing? Well, let's take care of that one, and that one, and that one, and that one. How many blades of grass and how many shadows are there within this being that seem to be overlaid upon the Self?" Does it matter? You are busy birthing Christ!

What happens when that really occurs? First—and listen well—*nothing will be unacceptable to you.*

Yet, the mind still resists, "Well but, does that mean if somebody is not a vegetarian that they're still loved? Does that mean if somebody votes for someone I am sure is the wrong guy that they're not insane, that I can love them? Does that mean that someone who seeks power and, therefore, creates a war and kills five thousand women and children, that I can still look upon them and not have my love be disturbed? Does it mean that whatever arises within this temporary world is really, truly, literally, not a problem for me any longer—that *nothing* is unacceptable?"

Yes. It does not mean you condone it. It means it is no longer unacceptable. For what you cannot accept, you will judge. And every judgment is the attempt to *murder* what you have decided has no right to be.

Judgment is the opposite of forgiveness. It lives on the side of the fence with fear. Forgiveness lives on the side of the fence with Love, and only Love can heal this world. Imagine, then, living in a state of being in which literally nothing was unacceptable to you because you knew that the Source of your true being was far beyond the limitations of anything created in space and time. That not even death, which has been created out of the contraction known as fear, is unacceptable.

I say unto you: If you will choose to trust me, I will show you the way to peace. I will wait for your reply as I can do nothing to take from you the freedom required to become wholly committed to allowing Christ to be birthed where once a

Lesson 7: Birthing the Mind of Christ

useless illusion reigned. I will show you how to become the being out of which all of creation is arising so that you will know the Truth that sets you free.

Now, this will raise up within you the most fundamental of fears possible. What is that? It is the last to be overcome: the fear of death. For when you are confronted by the Truth, you know that everything you have sought to create as a substitute for the Truth must die. That is why it is said, "The last to be overcome shall be death"— fear of death. Death is *allowed* that Christ might live.

Understand well: There is no one and there shall not at any time be anyone who reads these words to whom I have not given this promise unto. *I will show you the way to the Truth that is true always and sets you free.*

But only you can make the decision to bring the whole of your being to that journey. And all it requires is what you call a smidgen of willingness. A smidgen of willingness is all it takes.

I know the way home because I have completed the journey, and I will show you the way. With every word that I utter, my one intent is to reveal to you the place within you that is the presence of Love that you seek.

What if you chose to actually commit yourself to considering what I am sharing, and return to the innocence of a child, as you contemplated what it would mean in your life? Rest assured, when the journey *to* the Kingdom is completed, the journey *within* it begins anew. The bliss, the wisdom, the creativity, the laughter, the friendships, the family, the joy, the serenity, and the peace—that have been, for the most part, seen as an impossible dream—will become your most ordinary state of being. Yet, none of it can occur through any power that can move through *me*.

I can guide you. I can show you the way. And I can walk beside you on the way that you have chosen. At times, I can give you my strength until yours is as certain as mine, by carrying you. But ultimately, you must *demand* that I put you down so that *your* feet touch the soil of the Kingdom of Heaven and *you* walk, under *your* strength, under *your* certainty, beside me.

You will indeed find in that day and hour that as

Lesson 7: *Birthing the Mind of Christ*

often as you ask it of me, I will ask you, "How do you think we could do this? What would you like to create with me?" And then, indeed, we are as brother and brother, sister and brother, friends, dancing and playing in the Kingdom prepared for us of our Father.

One little shadow cast by a tiny blade of grass is all that seems to prevent you from coming wholly to where I am. If you tarry yet a little longer, it is all right. You cannot prevent me from knowing the Truth about you and loving you. When you are in Love, when you are so immersed in simply loving, is it not true that you have no sense of time at all? There is no sense of any effect disturbing your peace. You are just "swaying to the music." You are loving, and your wholeness grows even more holy.

Therefore, Love one another as I have loved you. For the Father has first loved me that I might show you the truth of what Love is and the reality of your being. I will not cease in doing this, regardless of how long you choose to tarry. For Love is, indeed, patient and kind. Love is not deluded, and Love does not allow delusion. Love embraces all things, trusts all things, and allows all things. It knows perfectly well where it is going, and never ceases in that journey until every blade of grass is released from casting shadows, and the whole of creation is returned to the Heart of God.

> Learn to love your Self and
> cry out to this world:
> I and my Father are one!
> That is the soil from which I move
> and live and have my being.
> So be it!

Always remember that the Father looked upon His only creation and said, "Behold, it is very good!" That goodness has a name and it is yours! And behold, it is very good! That light deserves to shine!

The doorway stands before you. Will you open it through the *power* of your choice? For what you experience will reveal to you what choice you have made this day.

Lesson 7: *Birthing the Mind of Christ*

Beloved and holy friends, may peace be with you always. And may the Truth that is true always shine within your hearts and minds throughout all ages. Remember, there's a perfectly good reason why I keep saying, time and again, "I am with you always." Amen.

LESSON 8

DROPPING PEBBLES INTO THE POOL OF AWARENESS

As always, I come forth as your equal—to abide with you, to walk with you, to communicate with you—from that Mind and that Heart which we eternally share as one, that Mind which is alone the reality of our *shared* Sonship, our shared existence. As always, I come forth in joy and also with humility. For I cannot join with anyone unless they provide the space within their consciousness and bid me enter therein.

Therefore, understand well, that when I come to abide with you, I come with a humility born of the recognition of the great mystery that has given you your existence. That mystery I have called Abba, Father.

Why? You have not come forth from some mechanical, unthinking force. You have come forth from pure Intelligence. You have come forth from pure Love. You have come forth from

Lesson 8: *Dropping Pebbles Into the Pool of Awareness*

a Source beyond all comprehension. You have come forth from the radiance of a Light so bright that the world cannot see it or contain it. You have come forth from that which, alone, is eternally real. Because you have come forth from it, you are one with it, always.

This means that you abide in a relationship—created to Creator, offspring or child to parent—that is so *intimate*, a bond *so deep*, that it cannot be broken at any time. As a wave that arises from an ocean cannot be separated from the ocean itself, so too, in each and every moment in your experience, do you abide in a union so powerful, so mysterious, so intimate and immediate that the mind cannot comprehend it.

This union connects you as the created with the mystery beyond comprehension that contains every drop of wisdom and intelligence necessary to create consciousness itself. Consciousness—the power to be aware, the power to choose—is what you truly are.

If this Source, this mystery, can birth this most fundamental aspect of creation, does it not deserve to be called Abba or Father, that which creates like unto itself? Can you, then, begin to feel, to know—not just as an intellectual idea, but as a lived reality, a knowingness—that if you are aware in this very moment, it is because you are one with the Source of all creation and cannot be separated from it in any way or at any time?

Fear, as we have said many times, is like a contraction. Again, if you were to imagine a wave arising from the ocean and then going into contraction because it thinks it is separated from its source, that contraction literally squeezes the life, the very flowing waters, out of that wave. Could that wave possibly continue when its very life force has been squeezed from it? Does it not then become mere drops of water fading from view, only to dissolve back into the ocean itself? Its radiance lost, never to be seen again.

If it were possible for the wave of your consciousness to truly have its life force squeezed out of it, you too would fade away as droplets returning to the ocean, never to be remembered or seen again.

Listen, and listen well: *that* would be death. But in reality, you are alive, always. Even when you

Lesson 8: *Dropping Pebbles Into the Pool of Awareness*

have identified yourself with the great constriction that fear is, your fears have never been able to squeeze out of you the great life force, the great reality, and the great gift of awareness. You have, therefore, never ceased to be. There has never been a time that you have not existed and there will never be a time when you will cease to be.

You are therefore, very much like a wave that has begun to arise out of an unseen ocean and as it gains momentum, it moves across the surface of a planet. Like the wave, you are in continual movement. Moving where? Into a forever extension of your awareness itself. Into a forever extension of whatever you choose to pick up along the way and make a part of your Self. Into a forever extension that will carry you into the experience or the fruits of the very thoughts you have held onto as your own.

Therefore, understand well: Right now, in this lived moment, wherever you are, whatever you are experiencing, all that you see, all that you feel, all that you know, all that you seek to avoid, and all the things you value and devalue, all things are contained *within* your awareness. For if they are not found there, they do not exist for you.

Therefore, look upon that which resides within your awareness, within your consciousness. What are the things that you *know* that you know? What are the things that you would avoid? What are the feelings that you have not explored? What are the objects, the people, the places, the values that you strive for, that seem to thrill even the cells of the body? What is the body itself, if not that which arises within your awareness?

Look at the planet around you. Look at every object in your room. Look at every thought you choose to think. Look at the perceptions and ideas that you defend so vociferously. Look at the thoughts and the feelings of others that make you cringe or wish to withdraw from them.

These things abide within you like the very power or life force of the wave that has arisen from the ocean. All of these things you have picked up along the way. And the way has been very long and varied indeed! If you can imagine never ceasing to exist, it means that you have been as a wave of awareness, passing through every time frame, every planetary system, and every dimension of creation.

LESSON 8: *Dropping Pebbles Into the Pool of Awareness*

Along the way, one thing has remained constant. You have been in constant relationship with *all* of creation. Oh yes, you may select out a few people, a few objects, a planet, a dimension, and focus all of your attention there. Attention is nothing more than the decision of what you are going to use the power of your awareness to focus on. It seems that you have excluded everything else, but that is like an optical delusion of consciousness.

While it is very true that you have *selected out* aspects of creation to focus your attention on, yet underneath—in the depth of the wave that is unseen by the physical eye, unseen by your conscious awareness or your day-to-day mind—you have remained in perfect communion with *all* of creation.

You are, therefore, in relationship with all created things, and there is a communication that occurs without ceasing. Imagine being able to look into the air of your planet and to literally see the radio waves, the television waves, and all of the electrical waves that keep bouncing back and forth across your planet. This is what you swim in daily. Your consciousness pervades this field of vibrations.

The Way of the Heart

You Only Experience What You Have Chosen to Create

You are the one who selects out what you are going to be aware of, what you are calling into your lived experience. You *select* what is going to make an imprint upon you.

Imagine, then, a pool of clear, still water. Into it you drop a solitary pebble. From the pebble there radiates waves. This is what is occurring *constantly* in the field of your wave of awareness.

As you have attracted to yourselves certain persons, places, things, objects and above all, thoughts, beliefs and perceptions, you have dropped them like little pebbles into the still clear pool of your vast and eternal awareness. What you experience are the effects, or the ripples, of those pebbles. They literally join with the other ripples that you have created. As these ripples move out and touch one another and come back to you, this is the field of creation that makes up your physical, third-dimensional reality.

You are, therefore, never experiencing anything except what *you* have chosen to create through

Lesson 8: *Dropping Pebbles Into the Pool of Awareness*

your selection of the pebbles that you have dropped into the field of your awareness. You literally never experience a solitary thing. You do not experience objects. What you experience is the *effect* of a thought or a belief in objects. You never experience another person, for they also are made up of a whole web of vibrations.

You could say that each person, each object is really a field of relationships, unique and seemingly different from you, but a web of relationships nonetheless.

For what child can be separated from their parents, from their cultural background, from the unique experiences that they have had as they have interacted with the webs of relationship that have been around them since the moment of their conception? What kitten can be separated and singled out from the matrix of its mother and father? What leaf on a tree is separate from the temperature of the air, the quality of water and nutrients that come to it from the very soil of the Earth?

Everything is a web of relationship. All webs are in relationship with all other webs and they become grander and grander and grander ad infinitum.

You are a web of relationships out of which you have selected *certain* pebbles—whether they be thoughts or perceptions or experiences—and you have dropped them into the still clear pool of your awareness in order to create even more ripples. Then, you have chosen which ones will have the greatest value for you. These you *lock* in to your being and they become your emotional field. The emotional field is the first level of crystallization of the body.

From the emotional field, a further crystallization creates the appearance of a physical form. It is that which you push around the planet in your very temporary third-dimensional form of attention, while all around you—and just beneath the level of your conscious daily awareness—you remain in communication with all webs of relationship throughout all dimensions of creation. It is for this reason that an inspiring thought can come suddenly to you and penetrate your daily awareness. And you wonder, "Where did that thought come from?"

Or suddenly a picture appears in your mind. It could be of anything—a man and a woman making love, a man and a man making love, a

Lesson 8: *Dropping Pebbles Into the Pool of Awareness*

child playing in a park, a dolphin, or a picture of conflict or war. Where did it come from?

Because you live in perfect communion, and you are like a grand field of energy in which all webs of relationship are reverberating constantly, you actually have access to the complete entirety of creation. And this entirety of creation is not limited to what is occurring now, as you understand time. You have available to yourself everything, which you would call the past and the future.

These things are available to you at all times. There is not one of you who has not experienced this for yourself. Perhaps you suddenly thought of a friend, and then the telephone rang, and you knew it was that friend.

It makes no sense in your causal third dimensional plane, but because underneath—even though your conscious mind was busy making breakfast and wondering about which stocks to buy and sell, or which perfume to put on the body—you remain in perfect communion. It is why, when there is a deep resonance between friends separated by thousands of miles, all of a sudden you know they need you to call them.

You feel a sense of concern. Maybe they just stubbed their toe, but you pick up the vibration.

You all live this. You all know this. There is no secret about it. What I would seek, then, to attract your attention to is one of the pebbles that has been dropped into the field of your awareness, which is generally true for virtually everyone involved in the third dimensional experience called physicality.

Imagine a sentence being dropped from a vast height, picking up speed until it strikes the still pool of your awareness and sends a ripple out, creating a vibration through you. The sentence is simply this: "It is not possible for me to have complete mastery over which pebbles are dropped into my awareness for I am at the mercy of the vibrational field set up by the ripples of all of the thoughts and webs of relationship in which I swim constantly."

That perception is absolutely true…as long as you choose to believe it. That perception or belief is absolutely laughable and powerless as soon as you choose to acknowledge that this is so.

What is the point of that? It is simply this: If you

Lesson 8: Dropping Pebbles Into the Pool of Awareness

would choose to awaken wholly, if you would choose not just to be a wave that has mysteriously arisen from the ocean, if you would choose to be more than just another soul that has arisen from the Mind of God and is, somehow, crashing about through the universe, it is *absolutely necessary* to own, as your own, the pebble that drops into the still, clear pool of your awareness with the thought:

> I am the one who chooses the effects
> I experience.
>
> I, alone, interpret all neutral relationships
> or experiences.
>
> I, alone, place the value upon objects,
> things, thoughts, and belief systems.
>
> I, alone, am the literal creator of my
> moment-to-moment experience.

This, as you can see, changes everything. Never again can you allow yourself to feel as though you are merely a victim of unconscious forces. Never again can you look out beyond yourself and find fault with another. Never again can the energy of blame be projected from you to be dumped upon another. Never again can the energy of judgment hold sway in your holy mind. This thought, this one singular pebble dropped into the still pool of your awareness is absolutely essential if you would decide to awaken wholly. And that is what this lesson is about.

You Are Not a Victim of the World You See

Though you would hear the word—that which carries the vibration of truth—many times, it can be denied as many times as it is heard. You can choose to not allow it to settle deep into that pool of awareness, so that it affects every drop of water that makes up the wave that you are. You can hold on to the hope that you are still a victim of the world that you see, that events hold some value in themselves that do not come from what you place upon them. And as long as you *choose* to deny the world, you cannot be set free.

For the mind that chooses, in even a small part, to perceive itself as a *victim* of its world of experience, remains powerless. It remains in a state that generates frustration, weakness, fear, self-doubt, unworthiness, suffering, pain, emotional pain of aloneness or separation from others, and lack of fulfillment. Ultimately, it

Lesson 8: *Dropping Pebbles Into the Pool of Awareness*

generates the echo of the belief that you have been squeezed so tightly by fear that you are literally separated from the ocean of the Mind of God.

Awareness is all that you have and all that you are. Out of your use of it, comes all that you choose to experience. And out of *that* comes your decision of *how* you will experience what you have called to your self.

In truth—and please listen well—no experience you have ever had has defined you or identified you. No experience you have ever chosen to create, to call to your self, and then to value as you valued it, has *ever* made you higher than or less than any one else—not even me. Although there are many who still need to believe that I am far beyond them. No experience you have ever had has proven your unworthiness to be supported, to be loved, by your Creator.

Therefore, you remain as you are created to be: a wave filled with the very self-same power as the ocean itself, a wave, a soul, a web of relationship arising from the holy Mind of God with the momentum to flow on forever with the freedom to create by deciding which vibrations you will allow to settle in and become a part of you, which thoughts you will defend, which perceptions you will cleave unto.

You are, then, eternally a creator. And this is the one thing that you have no free will about. You can never decide to be a non-participant in the very mystery of creation's extension. When you hold the thought, "I refuse to participate in God's creation," you have literally created the perception, the experience of yourself as being outside or separate from creation itself. You have created the insane emotion of trying to separate the wave from the ocean itself. And you *will* create the perception of separation, even though nothing, in reality, has been affected.

Why is this important? Because, you see, the process of healing is not difficult. It requires only your willingness to accept that you are the *effect* of the Creator's desire to create like unto itself—just as a wave is the effect of the ocean's desire to express itself in a new way, a new form, and to bring a uniqueness to every wave that arises from its mysterious depths.

Surrender, then, is the process in which you finally

relent; you give up resisting the fact of your very existence. You stop whining about it. You stop lamenting it. You stop worrying about it. You make the decision to get on with being alive! And what is alive about you is going to be alive forever. There is no place to hide and nowhere to go.

Creating as Christ

When you drop the pebble into the mind:

> I am not a victim of the world I see.
>
> I am a ceaseless creator, made and of one substance with my Creator itself.

Then, indeed, the questions begin to take a different shape. You begin to use the power of your awareness to deliberately and selectively choose which vibrations, which webs of relationships, you are going to pull into your field of awareness—which ones you are going to resonate with and which ones you are going to let dissolve from your mind, from your awareness.

If you have held onto a thought of smallness, a thought of lack, or a thought of powerlessness, now you begin to see that it is perfectly neutral. It is perfectly safe to look upon everything you have ever created and experienced and say, "It is very good, and now I'm done with it.

"What's next? What pebbles can I drop into my holy mind in this very moment? Can I look upon the current experience I'm having and see that it's nothing but the effect, the ripple, of a pebble or a thought that I dropped into my mind so long ago that I don't even remember it? Can I look upon those events that are unfolding around me…"

And if they are unfolding in your body, trust me, that is still *around* you, for you are much more than just the body.

"Can I begin *now*, am I willing *now*, to drop a different pebble into the still and infinite clarity of the pool of awareness that is what is alive about me always? Dare I think a different thought? Dare I drop such a pebble into my consciousness?"

So what pebbles could they be?

> I think I'll become a world savior, a Christ. What would that be like? What vibrations would I need to let go out of my life and which ones would I need to open to? What would it feel like? What would I see as I look out through the field of my awareness at creation?

LESSON 8: *Dropping Pebbles Into the Pool of Awareness*

> I think I'll allow myself to be able to commune with any web of relationship, any soul, any being, that exists on any plane of creation. Why, perhaps I'll even allow myself to know that I can be in communication with Jeshua.
>
> How wealthy can I become in this third-dimensional reality? How many golden coins could I possibly create in order to give them away to others?
>
> How many places on the planet could I take the body to in the span of one short physical life?
>
> How many beings could I say "I love you" to? How big can I make my heart be? How deep can I experience peace?

The realm of possibilities is as infinite as you are. The ones you select and choose are the ones that will create the web of relationships that you will call your life, your experience, even right down to the quality of how you will experience the transition—mistakenly called death—in your world.

Would you call it a death when you leave one room and close the door behind you and step into another room? Of course not. You just say, "I was there; now I am here." That is all that truly occurs when the molecules you have called to yourself are unglued because you release your value of them, and their constituents, their parts, dissolve back into the dust or the energy field of the planet. You merely leave one room and step into another.

What I call you to in this lesson is this: to be willing to allow the pebble to be dropped into your field, or pool of awareness, that carries the energy of the thought:

> From this moment forward, I elect
> to birth a Christ, and thereby
> learn what Christ is!

And your experience becomes the unfolding learning of what Christ is. When that learning completes itself, you discover that what you have learned is what you are created to be. You have returned full circle. The prodigal son or daughter, journeying through the field of all possibilities, has returned as the awakened Christ, and has taken up his or her rightful place at the right hand of the Creator.

LESSON 8: *Dropping Pebbles Into the Pool of Awareness*

What does all that symbolism mean? It just means you finally think only with your right-mindedness. You think as God thinks, and God thinks lovingly. God thinks infinitely, timelessly, patiently, certainly, and above all, God thinks *playfully*—full of play!

When you feel such Love and such joy welling up within you that you can hardly contain it, do you not start dancing and moving the body about, saying, "Oh, my gosh, what am I going to do with all this energy?" And you call your friends and say, "Let's have a party, let's go to a movie, let's create a delicious feast. Who could I write a letter to? Oh, who could I send flowers to?" Do you not become caught up in the desire to let some energy expand out of you, to touch all parts of your creation?

Well, imagine being God—infinite, vast, without a top or a bottom or a left or a right, filled with nothing but pure, unconditional, radiant Love! Can you imagine being able to contain yourself and say, "Oh, well, I think I will just sit here in this and not let anybody notice it"? No! God said, "Let there be light!" And it was very good! God looked upon all of creation, which literally means not just this planet, but all of an infinite number of creations of dimension upon dimension upon dimension, and all little webs of relationships called souls that He brought into existence in one split second and said:

> Lo, it is very good! This is My play! My joy and My Love and My aliveness have poured forth and overflowed My Grand Being and brought forth into manifest creation—you!

You—each and every one of you—are made of the very substance of that overwhelming Love and playfulness that has the power to create infinitely and thereby to extend creation itself! That is who you are! That is where you find yourself *now*, and now, forever. And you will never escape it.

Creating Mastery

Mastery comes when fear has been completely dissolved. Fear is dissolved not by fearing it, not by hating it, not by judging it. But by being looked upon with perfect innocence. Embraced in the same way that a scientist would watch the ripples of a little pebble that has been dropped into a pool of water to see how they have created

LESSON 8: *Dropping Pebbles Into the Pool of Awareness*

other ripples, and other temporary disturbances in the field or the surface of the water.

As you look within and notice the things you have become afraid of and how fear has constricted your creativity, your joy, your playfulness and your unlimitedness, you merely look with innocence and wonder and say, "Oh, I see how that ripple has affected the creation that I call my life. Do I like it? Not any more. Good! I think I'll be rid of that. What can I replace it with?"

Mastery is a state in which you have embraced yourself as a ceaseless creator and assumed complete responsibility for everything that comes into the field of your awareness *without judging it*, so that you can simply decide whether it is going to stay or be dissolved in its effects. Mastery is fearlessness. That is, you no longer fear the infinite, creative power of your perfect union with God. "I and my Father are one!" is one expression of mastery.

If I, who uttered those words so long ago in your experience of time, can demonstrate to anyone who will look that consciousness transcends the limited beliefs about the body, life and death that the world seems so determined to defend at all costs, if I can demonstrate that only Love is real, if I can demonstrate the power to communicate with minds across creation, if I can bring forth creations by joining with other minds who may temporarily think they are just a body, such that written words fall upon a page and the page becomes part of a book that you are now reading, such that your heart is touched at just the right time, if I can do these things, so too can you. And indeed, greater things than these *shall* you do!

Beloved friends, is it not time to assume complete responsibility for the grand freedom that has been imparted to you by Abba, Father, Creator, Source of your being? Is it not time to begin spending time disengaging from your entangled view that holds you to believe that what you feel and what you think is the *effect* of all of the energies and things that are coming *at* you, from around you? Is it not time to begin to use time to decide which pebbles you will drop into the field of your awareness consistently, day by day, hour by hour, and even breath by breath?

For these things create your tomorrows, and you cannot ever escape the reality that you are, and

Lesson 8: *Dropping Pebbles Into the Pool of Awareness*

always will be, in the process of creating your tomorrows. Death will never separate you from it. Denial does not change it.

You are free to decide what your tomorrows will be through the act of seeking first the Kingdom. This means to rest into that inner silence in which you *know* that you are a wave having arisen with perfect momentum out of the depth of the ocean of God's holy Mind. And that what you carry with you is the result of the thoughts and the beliefs and the perceptions—like pebbles—that you have dropped into the wave of your awareness.

This very process is what created you, and this very process is how you have always created. If you have ever received an education, how did you end up with your body in a classroom? Did somebody kidnap you and sit you down and say, "Here, you must learn these things"? No. You first held a thought, a picture, and you placed a value upon it, and you attracted the means that carried you into the lived experience of receiving the education that *you* had decided upon.

What relationship have you ever entered out of lack of awareness? None. You dropped the pebble into the mind that said, "I want relationship with another being, another body, another place upon the physical planet." You have always been doing it, and you have always experienced the fruit or the effect of the quality of vibration of the pebble that has created the ripples that have become your experiences. In reality, your experience, that is, your awareness—what is true about you—is no different than what is true about me.

The only difference has been that I learned to train myself, hour by hour, to drop only *unlimited* pebbles, that send out vibrations of unconditional acceptance and Love, forgiveness, unconditional and unbridled vision and revelation, while *you* have selected to do that only a *few* times.

Then you rush back and pick up the pebbles of unworthiness, or limitation, or lack, or fear, or smallness, and you drop ten or twelve quick ones in. Then you go back to the other cupboard and say, "Hmm, here's the pebble that says, 'I and my Father are one'… oh, had enough of that!" And back you go again.

While I stay on this side of the fence saying:
I and my Father are one!

Lesson 8: *Dropping Pebbles Into the Pool of Awareness*

> I and my Father are one!
> I am an unlimited being forever!
> How many universes can
> I be the savior of today?

You, on the other hand, have said, "That sounds very good. I and my Father are one. Oh, here is a pebble that says my car needs to break down today."

This is all there is! Which side of the fence are you going to sit on and drop the pebbles from? Which tree will you eat the fruit thereof? The tree of knowledge of good and evil?

Use that symbolism well, for when you drop the pebble in the pond it is like saying, "Well, I think I will take a bite of this piece of fruit. Oh, but it's so sweet, it's so good and so perfect. I'd better have a bite of a rotten one too to balance it out." The tree of good and evil—positive and negative, unlimitedness/limitation, forgiveness/judgment, love/fear—is like holding a beautiful flower and seeing the petals and saying, "Oh, it's so beautiful. I can't quite take it, so I think I'll prick my finger on the thorn and bring myself back down."

No one ever told you, and your Creator never insisted, that you eat of the tree of good and evil.

For all *good fruit* has been given you freely. And you are always free to choose *which* fruit you will eat thereof:

> I and my Father are one! What a blessed creation. I have been having so much fun as this wave. Yes, I see what I have carried along with me. Well, it was fun. I gained a few things. Now, what's next?
>
> Unlimitedness—kerplunk! Perfect Love— kerplunk! Wealth—kerplunk! The ability to heal—kerplunk! kerplunk! kerplunk!
>
> Oh, yes, I see that little pebble over there sitting on the shore that I have picked up a million times: unworthiness—kerplunk! But no more! Be done with you!
>
> I and my Father are one! I and my Father are one! Father, create through me the good, the holy, and the beautiful, for this is the reason for my being! How big of a wave can I become? How powerful can I become? How radiant can I become? How much of You can I express through me? Kerplunk!

Remember well, you are creating your tomorrows *now*! And what you experience never comes to

LESSON 8: *Dropping Pebbles Into the Pool of Awareness*

you from outside your Self. If you worry over lack of golden coins—kerplunk! And you begin to attract the vibrational ripples that will *seem* to picture back to you, reflect back to you, the truth that you have chosen to believe, "I live in lack and I can't get out. (kerplunk!) I can't possibly talk to Jeshua. I'm not worthy." (kerplunk!)

And the vibrational waves that come to you are the static that restricts your ability to transcend the third dimension and plug into others. So that even if I yell and shout, "Hey, I am talking to you, listen," your mind says, "That's not possible because I've dropped a rock in (kerplunk!) that says, 'It's not possible' and therefore, I do not hear a thing."

Do you begin to get the picture? Do you begin to *feel*, in the core of your beingness, the essence of this lesson's message? You cannot escape being what you are created to be. In each and every moment you are, literally, using that ceaseless and unlimited power to create. And you remain perfectly free at any time to create anew. What you will experience in your tomorrows is only the effect of which pebbles you are choosing to drop into the field of your awareness as thoughts *now*.

So the only question is this:

> Am I, as a creative being made in the image of God, willing to deliberately, consciously, and actively choose being responsible for which thoughts, which pebbles, are dropped into my mind in each moment?

If the answer is "yes," ask:

> What do I want the new pebbles to be? What vibrational qualities will I call to myself and thereby create my tomorrows?

Any time you react to what you believe is outside of yourself—you may be absolutely *positive* of this—you have elected to pick up that old pebble that says, "I'm a victim of the world I see. What I experience is caused by forces outside of me. The fault really is in my mother, my brother, my father, my partner, my child. The fault really is in the government, and the planet, and the quality of air. The fault really is from a source outside of me, and I have no choice, but to react to it." To which I can only say:

> Would you rather be right or happy?

Indeed beloved friends, consider well the essence of this lesson's message. For upon this, we will

LESSON 8: *Dropping Pebbles Into the Pool of Awareness*

begin to build as we move toward the ending of The Way of the Heart. This is but a foundation from which those that are willing can spring forth into a grander dimension, a grander experience of living as a deliberate co-creator with God.

But it all begins with a need to be responsible for *owning* the truth of the message of this lesson. For without that, there can be no change in your consciousness and, therefore, in what you will experience in your tomorrows. So if there is something in your present that makes you shudder, just think what is waiting for you if you once again deny choosing this responsibility and the power that comes with it.

Beloved and holy friends, remember that I come not to bring peace to the world, but to shake it up so that those beings that make up the world can discover where true peace is truly hidden—*within themselves*. And where Heaven abides—*within themselves*. And where Christ lives—*within themselves*.

Peace then, be unto you always. Amen.

Lesson 9
All Events Are Neutral

I am your brother and your friend, who looks upon you and sees naught but the face of Christ within you. Christ is the firstborn of the Father. That is, it is that which is begotten, and not made. Christ is God's creation. Christ is the holy Child of God. Christ is as a sunbeam to the sun, radiating forever from the holy Mind of what I have called Abba.

Therefore, I come forth to abide with you in perfect joy, and in perfect freedom, and in perfect reality. I come forth to join with that part of you that abides always in perfect knowledge, perfect peace, perfect knowingness, and in perfect union with your Creator.

I come not to speak of things that you do not know. I come not to use words that do not already abide within you. I come not with the wisdom that you do not already contain. I come not with a Love grander than that which already flowers within the silent places of your own

Lesson 9: *All Events Are Neutral*

heart. I come *not* to place myself above you. I come only to walk as an equal beside you.

I come because I love you. I come because I am your friend. Of all the things that I could possibly choose to do with the unlimited power of consciousness given equally unto me of my Father as it was given unto you, of all of the places and dimensions and worlds in which I could reside in this moment, I come to abide *with you* to bridge the gap that seems to yet separate you from me.

In reality, all dimensions of creation reside in a space far smaller than the tip of a pin. In reality, all dimensions of creation are so vast that you could never measure them. In reality, there is no gap between where you are and I am. This is why I can be no further from you than the width of a thought. But oh, beloved friends, the power of a thought is the power to create universes, and within universes to create yet more universes, and within those universes to create world upon world upon world upon world upon world.

Your lived experience is that momentarily your attention seems to be focused on your unique world, which shares some things in common with many other beings. You have what is called in your world a consensus reality—we would say a consensus *experience*—born out of a universal reality. Beloved friends, even as you abide in your awareness in this moment, you are the creator of the world you experience. And you do this in so many ordinary ways. When you stand face to face with anyone and for just a split second, you alter the position of the body through which you gaze upon them—you take up a new stance, a new perspective—in that very split second, you have created a new experience for yourself.

When you look upon a friend, and the mind moves from neutrality (which is where you begin every experience) into the thought, "That is my friend, Mary. That is my friend, St. Germain. That is my friend, Peter. That is my friend, Joanna. That is my friend, Nathaniel." Whatever the name may be, when you hold that thought, already you begin to change the experience.

You are a literal creator in that moment. For when you name anything, you define it according to the factors that you have built into the name that you use. When you look upon a field of energy arising from the mystery of Earth and

Lesson 9: *All Events Are Neutral*

you say the word "tree," instantly you have brought forth into your manifest experience everything you have ever decided is associated with the field of energy that you have called tree. In this way, your experience is entirely unique. It has never been before; it will never be again. Nothing can repeat it. This is why creation is forever new.

Yes, you can stand with your friend and look upon a tree and nod your head and say, "Of course, that's a tree. Yes, I see the branches. I see the leaves." But as soon as you have named it, you have brought forth all of the associations you have called to yourself, your experience of that field of energy that you have called tree. Rest assured, those called environmentalists and those that you have labeled loggers definitely see a different experience though they both use the same word tree. Which is right, then, and which is wrong? This does not apply.

In this lesson, we want to address another of the important pebbles that you must drop into the clear, still pool of your awareness. It is simply this: All webs of relationship, all energy fields, are *absolutely neutral*. What creates experience is how you decide you will view that web of relationship, that field of energy. The *effect* of that decision is also completely neutral.

But how can that be? For when a logger sees a tree and sees only the profit to be made, forests disappear. And when an environmentalist looks at a tree, the tree remains and the mighty owls and the birds have a place to make their home. Surely, are we not to perpetuate the same reality, the same experience that all human beings have had? Is there not loss when the forest disappears? Listen well and carefully: All events are neutral. You are the one that places the value upon it.

Now, does that mean that one should become cold hearted, unconscious, and blind to their actions? Of course not, for part of awakening means to realize one's interconnection with the web of all relationships. It means awakening a reverence for the mystery that is Life. But it also means to release judgment of another who would view the tree differently. For you see, the body that you have crystallized out of a field of infinite energy has but one purpose. It is a communication device.

Lesson 9: *All Events Are Neutral*

Therefore, let your primary perception, your primary guiding light in your third dimensional experience be this:

> What do I choose to communicate to the world with every gesture, with every breath, with every word spoken and with every decision made?

For ceaselessly, while the body lasts, you are engaged in the process of communicating to the world, making manifest to the world, what you have chosen to value, what you have called into your experience and imbued with value. This means that ceaselessly you are engaged in teaching the world what you believe holds the greatest truth, the greatest value.

When an environmentalist looks upon a logger, becomes exasperated and judges that logger or vice versa, the body is being used to communicate the value of judgment. That creates fear and contraction. The result of many, many minds choosing to value the right to judge is the effect you call your world, in which everything seems to be expressing conflict, struggle, "butting of heads" and the Armageddon of opposite ideas running into each other. And just beneath it all, all events remain completely neutral.

Even if the forests of your planet were completely taken away, that would be a neutral event. Why? Because if all of the trees were gone, if the very physical planet you call Earth died, dissolved from view, Life would continue. Life would merely create new worlds. It does it all the time. *You* do it all the time.

The events, then, that you experience are always neutral. What you see occurring in the world around you remains neutral until *you* make the decision what it will be—*for you*. You will name it and, therefore, you will define it. When you define it, you call all of the associations of that to yourself.

This is why once I taught it is very wise to forgive seventy times seven times. It was for a very selfish reason. If one wrongs you and you spend your energy convincing them that they have wronged you, that you have a right to be angry and to be attacking in any way, you call to yourself—even into the cells of the body—the energy of conflict, judgment, war, death, disease, unhappiness and separation *instantly!*

Lesson 9: *All Events Are Neutral*

But if you forgive seventy times seven, then in each of those moments of forgiveness, you call into your field of energy that which reminds you of unconditional Love, perfect peace, a power that transcends anything that arises in the world. You call to yourself the reality of Christ. And all of it hinges on nothing more than the pebbles that you drop into your mind.

Look with Innocence on What You Value

Where, then, have you drawn the line? Where have you said, "I will allow neutrality to all events in *this* sphere, but not in *that* sphere.

"If my friends divorce or separate, well okay, I'll see that as neutral. But if my spouse leaves me, that is not neutral. If my friend's father leaves three million dollars to his children, well, that's fine. That's a neutral event. But if my father leaves his three million dollars to charity and leaves me out of the picture, that is not a neutral event.

"If the streams in a country on the other side of the world from where I am become polluted because the consciousness of a community allowed a factory to be built without safeguards, well, it's on the other side of the world, a neutral event. But if they build it in my backyard, it is no longer neutral."

It is always wise to look lovingly to see where you have drawn the line, to see what you will look upon as neutral and what you cling to as being filled with meaning and value that is unquestionable. For there you will find what requires forgiveness within you. We have shared with you that mastery is a state of fearlessness. When you place a value upon something and then become adamant that that value exists in the event or the object outside of you, you have secured your place in fear. And fearlessness is as far from you as the east is from the west.

Look well then, to see where you have placed a value, and insisted that that value be unshakable. How many times in each of your days do you say, "Oh, boy! If my dog ever died I would not be able to take it. That would just be the end of me." Or "If the banks collapse…oh, God, I wouldn't be able to take that!"

Be careful what you decree. Look to see where

Lesson 9: *All Events Are Neutral*

you are emotionally enmeshed with the value you have placed upon anything or anyone. Any relationship whatsoever, whether it be the relationship with your spouse, the relationship with your body, the relationship with your cat or your dog, the relationship with your bank account, the relationship with your government—look at *all* of your relationships.

For you have made them what they are. Where can freedom be experienced, save within a consciousness that has learned how to transcend the contraction of fear? And fear is the result of your attachment to the values you have placed upon the events you experience, which are made up of events, persons, places, and things. All of these are actually just events.

Every web of relationship comes to you perfectly neutral. You decree it by naming it and defining it. When one comes to you in anger and you react, recognize that you first decided that they are angry, and you have brought forth with it all of the associations you have ever decided to value concerning what anger means.

Yet in that very moment, you hold the power to witness this field of energy circulating through the body and mind and the speech of another, and to see it as a dance of energy, a mystery arising from some unseen source and web of relationships. You could look upon it with curiosity and with wonder if you defined it differently.

This is true for all things that arise. Even the great diseases that seem to threaten the life of the body can be looked at with complete neutrality. But if you define them in a specific way, you will call to yourself the fear of that event, which comes with all of the associations you have learned from the world and from your own experiences.

The message of this lesson is simple, but it is very important. It builds on all that we have shared previously with you. You are a creator, and you cannot help but create. The question, then, is:

What will you create in each moment?

Far beyond the great thrill of the magic of creating events or objects in third dimensional reality are the *qualities* that you create, such as peace, unlimitedness, forgiveness, compassion, and wisdom. These too are creations.

LESSON 9: *All Events Are Neutral*

Compassion does not exist floating about in the universe until you manifest it and cultivate it within your own consciousness. Christ consciousness cannot be said to truly exist—for *you*—until you create it within yourself. Your union with God does not even exist—for *you*—until you decide to open to the lived experience of it. Much as a food you have never tasted might as well not exist for you until you journey to that country, purchase it and place it in the body. Or in your day and age, go to your grocery store and find the gourmet international section.

Nothing can be said to exist—for *you*—until you have tasted the lived experience of it. So when you hear talk about enlightenment, when you hear talk about union with God, when you hear talk about unconditional love, stop nodding your head thinking you know what these things are, and turn your attention within. Do you abide in a lived experience of these things? Immediately you will know the answer.

If your answer is, "No, I hear talk about enlightenment and I get little glimpses, but I don't really know what it is because I'm not feeling it completely in my lived experience," right away you will know that there must be something that you have valued *other than* enlightenment that you are insisting remains in place in your consciousness. What is it? Search it out, find it and decide whether you still want it.

We would perceive there are many in your world that like to walk around *as if* they are in a state of peace with smiles upon their faces. Perhaps they carry the Holy Bible in their hand or some other such text. They wear some religious icon upon their body so as to create the appearance of one who is at peace. But inwardly, they are not at peace. When they turn on their television and they watch how the logger has felled yet another tree, inwardly they respond by calling that one "ignorant" or "stupid" or "limited."

In that moment, they have spoken to the universe the truth that they are choosing to live, "I am not one who wants to know what peace is. I am not one interested in forgiveness. I am not one interested in wisdom. I am interested in judgment and the high that I feel in my body through the act of judging another as being less than myself."

Lesson 9: *All Events Are Neutral*

In short, it is time to give up the pretense. It is time to begin viewing yourself from the perspective of an absolute, ceaseless creator. Begin looking at exactly what you are creating in each moment of your experience. Bring the quality of childlike innocence to what you *actually* experience, not what you tell everybody else you are experiencing. It is time to become honest with the effects of the ripples of the rocks or the pebbles you have dropped into the field of your awareness as a great form of play.

For a creator who understands their infinite power to create and who understands that it is going on ceaselessly—that effects are being generated moment to moment to moment to moment that will indeed be making up their tomorrows—*gladly* gives up the energy of denial. And turns to look upon every moment of their experience that they might discern what choice they must have made to bring about the effects they are currently experiencing.

When a bill comes, and your body shakes and you go into contraction and worry because there are not enough golden coins in the checkbook to pay for it, the creator *stops* and looks upon all that is being experienced in the field of the body, in the emotional body and at the thoughts being held in the mind.

They begin to notice how they are viewing the objects around themselves, the world around them, in order to begin to wonder, "What thought must I have dropped into the pool of my mind to create the *effect* of lacking golden coins? And is that a thought I wish to drop into my mind so that I create similar effects in my tomorrows?"

Here is the doorway of wisdom. Do not create unconsciously and then just walk away. But learn ceaselessly from your creation. For in this way you begin the process of dissolving the creation of an un-enlightened being and you begin to build the creation of a Christ—here and now, in this moment.

The Power of Your Thoughts

Never, ever believe that your *thoughts* are neutral. I said earlier that events are neutral, but your thoughts are not. For your thoughts literally are imbued with the power of creation. They do not create neutrally. That is, every thought reverber-

Lesson 9: *All Events Are Neutral*

ates a quality of vibration that spreads out from you, touches the shores of manifested reality, and comes back to you. That is what you experience as the positive and negative events of your life.

Now, it is very true—please listen carefully to this—that at any moment as you go along in your experience, as you experience the reverberation, the coming back of the ripples you have sent out, in that very moment you are not a victim of what you have created. Because in each such moment you remain as perfectly free as you were when you first dropped the pebble into the pond that even created the ripple in the first place. You are free to choose how you will experience the effect of that ripple.

And if you experience it with unconditional freedom, with unconditional acceptance and Love, forgiveness, neutrality and innocence, you literally defuse the effects of that ripple upon the pool of your consciousness. And then, in that moment, you become instantly free to begin creating, in a new way, the ripples that you will experience in the future. And this is why you are never a victim of anyone's creation, especially your own.

It is not that life is so complex that you have created all these momentums and now you are stuck with them. In any moment that you *get it*, you can stop reacting as if you were a victim, and look merely at the ripples that are coming back to you that you have sent out from yourself and say:

> This has come into my field of experience as an awesome mystery. This means that I am an awesomely powerful being! Therefore, I will look lovingly upon this ripple.
>
> Yes, I know it needs to play itself out. But as it does so, I'm going to be wise enough to see the transparency of it, to see the lack of effect that it really has. It doesn't change who I am. It doesn't add anything to my life. It doesn't take anything from it. It merely is an experience called life passing through the field of my awareness.
>
> If I look lovingly upon it, if I embrace it, I can transmute it, and therefore, already be engaged in the process of creating a whole different kind of vibrational ripple that will create my tomorrows.

That means that while the power of your thoughts is not neutral, the events called the

Lesson 9: *All Events Are Neutral*

effects of those thoughts can be either neutral or not neutral, depending on how you use the very primary power of awareness. We are seeking to share with you how infinitely *free* you are.

There are many in your world that teach this illusory doctrine of what is called karma—that what you send out now you *must* experience sooner or later, and how you experience it is directly related to the quality of the ripple you send out. *That is not true.* That would make you a victim.

If you are made in the image of God, and I assure you that you are, you are not a victim of the world you see. You cannot, in reality, be victimized by anyone or anything at any time because your reality is that you are made in the image of God. If you could truly be victimized, it would mean that God creates *unlike Herself.* Does a salmon come from an oak tree? Does a nebula come out of the womb of a woman? Does a raspberry grow on a grocery store shelf? No. Like begets like.

Therefore, why would you ever believe that God—who is but Love and unlimited creativity and power—could ever beget something that is small and little and powerless? It does not happen. God cannot be victimized. Therefore, God's creation remains victimless.

All events remain neutral, and all that the environmentalist and the logger are doing is using the power of consciousness to momentarily create the belief that they are *this* and not *that*. They place a value of their own choosing upon an event of energy that they call a tree. And by what value they place upon it, they call the quality of experience they will have into their field of awareness. That is all that is happening.

The energy that makes up the tree is eternal forever. It may change form, but Life remains. Therefore, lament not the passing away of a species, but trust the Grand Intelligence that gave rise to it in the first place. For it is still busy creating even greater universes. This is why loss does not exist.

How does all of this relate to your daily experience? As we move into the lessons that follow, it is going to become *very* crucial that you have a foundation upon which to build.

LESSON 9: *All Events Are Neutral*

Five Minutes a Day — The Foundation of Mastery

If you are ready to completely assume responsibility for having been created in the image of God and that, therefore, you are an eternal creator, begin *now* to utilize some time each day, without letting a day go by, in which you sit with yourself. Not with your mate, not with your parents, not with the television, not with your favorite sport team, not with your favorite actor or actress, not with your favorite religion, not with your favorite god or master or savior, not even me. Sit with you. Start by acknowledging that you are one with God.

Understand that the very body that seems to have a heart within it beating Life for you is the effect of decisions and choices you have made. That the very chair that you are sitting on is the result of your attracting a web of relationships that is quite unique into your field of awareness called the physical universe. In this moment you are having an experience you have never had before. You are sitting in the chair now! The event is completely neutral. And nothing that you are experiencing in your consciousness exists or is sourced by anything outside yourself.

Give yourself five minutes to practice choosing how you will experience sitting in a chair. Will you do so with a mind full of worry, or a mind full of peace? A mind thinking of all the things it could be doing, or a mind *marveling* at how the weight of a body feels pressed against the seat of a chair? A mind that creates tension in the way the breath flows through the body, or a mind that creates ease and comfort?

Five minutes of practice sitting in a chair as an infinite creator of exactly what you are experiencing in your emotional field. Just that. You might even want to play with what it would feel like to sit in a chair *as a Christ*. What would that feel like? I will let you choose whether or not you would like to experience it. Five minutes each day. Do it without fail! Be with yourself, and decide how you will experience yourself *now*!

For you see, the *you* that sits down in the chair with whatever is going on in your consciousness—whatever feelings you are having throughout the body, whatever is going on in your primary rela-

LESSON 9: *All Events Are Neutral*

tionships, how the food is being digested in the body, all of it, the whole realm of your experience—is the effect of how you have been a million times when you have sat down to be with yourself in a thousand different chairs.

Utilize the very process of sitting down in a chair as a symbol of preparing the mind for the dropping of a pebble into it, out of which will reverberate the vibrations or ripples that will come back to you.

It is much easier to send out ripples and experience them when they come back in a blissful way, a way that brings you peace, joy, fun, laughter, play and unlimitedness, instead of having to constantly butt your head against something that you would rather transmute or run away from.

But it begins with five minutes, in which you acknowledge that you can create whatever experience you want, as a feeling that floods through your awareness, as a quality of thought that you allow to keep repeating in the mind.

You can sit in a chair as an awakened Christ—*now:*

> I and my Father are one!
> It's a beautiful day!

> I've manifested a physical form sitting in a chair in a corner of one little tiny dimension of creation.
> How amazing this moment is!
> I think I'll just sit here and feel the heart beating in the body and the breath flowing through it.
> Ah, there's the sound of a bird.
> I'm glad I called that to myself.
> What beautiful thoughts can I think right now? Who can I send Love to without lifting a finger?
> I am unlimited forever!
> I am free! I am free! I am free!

Do you think you would like to have that experience for five minutes? Why not begin today?

So many of you upon your physical plane keep searching for some form of magic that will bring the Kingdom of Heaven to you. You cannot bring it *to you*. You can only become aware of how you are using it to create the ripples that you send out *from yourself*. Do you know the saying in your world, "Wherever you go, there you are"? You *are* God's creation. You are in Heaven now.

Lesson 9: *All Events Are Neutral*

Heaven is not a place. It is a state of unlimited and infinite creative power because it is the reflection of God's holy Mind.

Why not be one who practices being the presence of Heaven? If that seems too awesome or too far beyond you, then just play with it for five minutes a day.

Trust me, I will love you no less if for the other twenty-three hours and fifty-five minutes you decide to play at pretending and feeling that you are little, unworthy, unloved, unloving, unlovable, that you are the scourge of the Earth and that life is constantly victimizing you. Go right ahead. I would never interfere with your free choice. I may not come and knock at your door, except for those five minutes. But you remain free to utilize time any way you wish.

For just five minutes, experience yourself as Christ, crystallizing a body as a temporary teaching and learning communication device, sitting in a chair in a totally neutral corner of creation because *you* want to have the experience of sitting blissfully at peace in your perfect knowledge of your union with God in this moment. You might even find yourself daring to have thoughts such as this:

> Well, since I am an infinite creator, what would I like to create for my tomorrows?

If during that five minutes, there is a knock upon the door and it is the bill collector, who cares? That is *that* soul's experience of thinking they are a bill collector and you are some bad person they must corral. Let them have their experience. Sit calmly, hear the knocking on the door and allow yourself to be entertained by the beautiful worlds you are creating for your tomorrows.

Here is the straight and narrow path that leads unto Life. Here is the eye of the needle through which you must pass. For it is not enough to just embrace the idea that "I am the creator of all that I experience." You must then choose to actively put it into practice. It begins with the practice of five minutes a day—that is all. When you feel that you can fulfill that for five minutes, then you can make it ten, and then twelve, and then fifteen, and then twenty.

You may respond, "You mean, for twenty minutes hang out as though I am Christ incarnate,

LESSON 9: *All Events Are Neutral*

totally in union with God, totally free to begin creating different ripples than I've ever experienced before, knowing that they will come back to me and become my manifested experience? With no doubt about it! But twenty minutes? Even if I could achieve that, that's such a small fraction of the time of a day."

Beloved friends, if you had faith as a tiny, tiny, tiny little seed, you would know that from that little tiny faith, you will create the mighty oak tree whose branches will shelter you from the blistering sun and give comfort unto many. Twenty minutes is an eternity when it comes to creating your tomorrows!

If you believe that the other twenty-three hours must be taken up by experiencing the effects of what you created a long time ago or the ripples that are coming back, so be it. Play with it. Let yourself transmute those moments.

For example, "Oh, here I am answering the door. Yes, bill collector. Hi, come on in. Have a glass of water. You know you're absolutely right, I didn't pay that bill. Do you want to know why? Silly me, I've actually decided to create the experience that I'm someone who can only create lack. That's why I have no money in my checkbook. It's just the darndest thing, isn't it?

"Oh, very good, you're going to turn my name over to the authorities, and now I'll have no credit with anybody on the planet. Well, go ahead if it makes your day. I have other things to do. I'm busy creating a new tomorrow. And I know that everything all around me is going to be taken from me anyway since everything birthed in time ends in time. My house will be gone, my car will be gone, my clothes will be gone and my friends will be gone. Everything I've experienced in time is changing anyway, so go ahead and take it from me now. It'll just speed up the process."

I do not speak of this tongue-in-cheek. I speak from the perspective of one who is an awakened Christ, who already *knows* how to birth universes to create that which is holy, good, and beautiful. I *know* that this is the way. It is the *only* way. Release the value you have attached to your experiences, even the bill collector, and spend your time instead deciding which pebbles you are going to drop into the field of your mind. For you will create as the result of what you choose

LESSON 9: *All Events Are Neutral*

to think today. And what you value today will show itself to you tomorrow.

I learned to value unlimitedness. I learned to value Love. I learned to value fearlessness. Yes, my method for doing that was rather unique, and I would not recommend that you follow in my footsteps. Unless, of course, you like the drama of being nailed to a cross and then stood up in front of all of your friends in order to learn to transcend fear in your mind!

I learned to value unbroken communication with every soul in every dimension of creation. I learned to value only my loving thoughts. And I birthed or grew a Christ out of the very seed of awareness that exists equally within each of you.

Therefore, in this moment, look around where you are. Look at the objects that you see. Look at the people that you see around you, if there are any. Notice whatever sounds may be coming into your field of awareness. Notice whatever pictures or ideas you may hold of what you are or what the world is. These are all fleeting and temporary illusions. They will pass away, and began passing away the moment they were created.

Therefore, indeed, beloved friends, look at all that is around you, and decide what value it holds for you. Will you see it as something that you *must* have in your existence? Or will you choose to see it as something you have playfully drawn to yourself; you appreciate it and it can be gone tomorrow and your peace will not be disturbed? Which way will you view the world?

Five minutes—one for each finger and thumb on a hand—in which you choose to sit as Christ in the midst of your kingdom, your creation. And *you* decide which thoughts you will hold and, therefore, determine how you see all that is in the field of your awareness, and which thoughts *you* will allow to begin to generate the ripples that you will send out that *will*—there is no way to escape it—return to you.

Planting the Seed that Produces the Desired Result

Once indeed there was a farmer who went out to plant the seed in his ground. But before he went to plant the seed, he selected the seed very carefully. The other farmers rushed out because they thought, "Oh, look, it is the time for the planting

Lesson 9: *All Events Are Neutral*

to begin. Everything is perfect. The conditions are just right. We must make haste and plant." And they bought whatever seeds they could get and went out and spread them across the ground, and began their busy work of doing what they had to do. Rest assured, they would have their harvest. But the wise farmer waited, and while he was laughed at by his colleagues, he carefully selected every seed. He waited until he could hold it in his hand and say, "Oh, I like the vibration of *this* seed. This feels very good. Oh yes! I can just see the beautiful plant that is going to arise from this. The fruit of it will be the sweetest in the valley."

And he gathered his seeds. He paid no attention to the passing of the dates on a calendar. He paid no attention to the changing weather conditions. He knew that when the time was right the seed would be planted, and from it would burst forth the flower of those seeds. He *knew* it! He gave no thought to the opinions of his colleagues. He enjoyed the process of loving the seeds that he was making his own.

Then the farmer went out and he cast the seed upon the soil of his farm, which is likened unto the soil of your own awareness. He planted the seeds, and he tamped them down, and he nurtured them, and he watered them, and he cultivated them with a smile upon his face.

And yes, the neighbors' seeds seemed to be already sprouting up through the ground. He could not have cared less, for he knew that *these* seeds would bring him an *eternal* harvest, that they would not just burst forth once from the soil, then throw out some mediocre fruit, and then die. For he had selected seeds that would constantly bring forth, in each season, the *best* of fruits. He loved them, and he nurtured them, and he cultivated them.

Long after the other farmers had grown weary and tired and had experienced drought, and seeds that brought forth fruit where insects would come and destroy them, that would not be purchased by the people in the market place, this one farmer became the greatest of farmers in the entire valley. People would come from all over the world to bite, to take a little nibble, out of the fruit that came from his garden.

Yet, the farmer merely delighted in continually

Lesson 9: *All Events Are Neutral*

loving and nurturing these seeds, and cultivating the soil in which they were planted daily. He never took his consciousness away from his perfect union with those seeds. He never once forgot that *he* was the one that created his farm as a direct result of his careful selection of which seeds he would plant in his soil. And while others marveled at his good fortune, and while others were jealous of his good luck, the farmer always knew that no magic was involved.

He merely followed in the footsteps of the wisdom given to him by God:

> "Take My fruit and plant it in your consciousness. Know that you are one with Me, and that fruit you experience is the result of the seeds you plant in your own consciousness. Know that you cannot help but experience the result, the fruit, of the seeds you plant. *Nothing* bursts forth on the vine of your experience by accident.
>
> "Therefore, create with Me, my child. Create like unto Myself, by knowing, *knowing* that you are a creator, a farmer, a planter. And you will, indeed, harvest the *quality* of the seeds that you plant.

"Just as you, beloved child, are the harvest of the seed I once planted, when first I held the thought of you in my holy Mind. And in that moment, you arose as a sunbeam from the sun, made in My image. I held you as the thought of Love in form. And I bestowed you with all good things.

"Therefore, see yourself as I see you. Embrace yourself as I embrace you. Accept yourself as you are—a creator, creating without ceasing.

"And just as I sat upon my throne (which means sitting in the center of All That Is), and beheld you as a loving thought, so too choose only to allow *loving* thoughts to enter into your consciousness. Choose to only allow loving thoughts to be expressed with your words. Choose only to allow loving thoughts to be translated into your gestures, your choices, and your actions.

"And thereby, create as I created you—that which extends joy forever, that which extends the holy, the beautiful, and the good forever. For that is what you are. That is how I thought of you when I created you.

Lesson 9: *All Events Are Neutral*

And that is what you remain eternally.

"Therefore, join with Me, by extending your creation, as I have extended you. Since you have manifested a physical body, accept my Son's teaching, and let that body be placed in a chair, that you might think like the Mind of Christ for five minutes. And you will beget an eternity that reflects the radiance of Heaven, just as you reflect My radiance when I look upon the unlimited soul that you are."

Indeed, in the entire valley there was but one farmer that was wise. Will *you* elect to join the union comprised of all of the hasty farmers? Or will you choose to take up residence as the *one* farmer who knows how to create wisely, and in faith, rests on perfect certainty, and merely sits back to wait for the ripples of Heaven to come and replace the ripples of hell, that once you created unwittingly?

Everyone is a minister. You cannot help but minister to the world in each moment. Therefore, begin your ministry of enlightened consciousness now! And I promise you this absolutely, irrevocably: *You will experience all that I have known and more!* You will experience complete victory over death. You will experience complete unlimitedness and abundance. You will experience perfect peace, perfect miracle mindedness, and perfect unbroken communion in bliss with all of creation!

Once when I was a man, I was taught to sit at the base of a tree for five minutes a day and to imagine myself to be the creator of all that I could think, all that I could see, and all that I could feel. Five minutes taken out of the hours of play of a child.

You are a child at play in your own kingdom. Will you give yourself five minutes to learn to be a Christ that creates in unlimited perfection in alignment with the Mind of God, whose experience is always radiantly blissful and free of limitation and fear? You *will* experience your creation. What that creation is, and how you experience it, is entirely up to you.

The message of this lesson, built upon the last, begins to translate the Truth into an action—very simple, very practical—so simple and so practical that you will be hard pressed to find a reason, an excuse, against it. For those of you so busy trying to take care of dealing with all the things life throws at

Lesson 9: *All Events Are Neutral*

you, even you know that you can find five minutes. And those five minutes can be the beginning of birthing a whole new universe for yourself.

And with that, peace be unto you always by making the decision to choose to receive peace as a Christ. Herein lies the secret of much of what will be shared in your upcoming lessons. For what I specifically seek to do in *The Way of Mastery* and this specific work you know and call as Shanti Christo, is the birthing of a multitude of Christs that dwell upon your Earth at the same time. It has never been done before!

Imagine a world with ten million awakened children of God—fully awake—not just as a belief or an idea, but who have mastered fear, who no longer live in doubt whatsoever, and who are busy creating universes that mirror perfectly the Kingdom of Heaven. Imagine it—if you dare!

It begins *now*. Practice well for the next thirty days. If not, you will find yourself having to go back and start anyway, before you can receive the next phase of what will be shared. The choice is yours.

Peace, then, be unto you always. Amen.

Lesson 10

The Way Is Easy and Without Effort

Beloved and holy children of Light and of Love divine, as always, I come forth to abide with you from that place which we share eternally as the one and only begotten son and of God. I am, therefore, *that Mind* which whispers to you in each moment of your inspiration. I am, indeed, *that Mind* that sneaks into your mind in the space between two fearful thoughts and reminds you of the Truth that sets you free.

Once I was a man — that is, just like you. I once turned my attention and became identified with a unique being that was birthed in time and faded away from time. And I walked upon your plane as all men and women do. But as I walked upon your planet, I began to ponder the meaning of creation, the purpose of my very existence.

And while others seemed to be gleefully caught up in or at least surrendered to the ways of the

LESSON 10: *The Way Is Easy and Without Effort*

world, seeking out their momentary distractions, their attempts to gain and control as much wealth as they could, and all of the rest, I would often wander off alone. I would sit beneath the trees beside a flowing stream to try to unlock the mystery that shows forth itself as the beauty of a flower, to try to see the power that revealed itself as the wind that would dance across the grasses, and to count the sparkling diamonds shimmering across the surface of a lake as the morning sun arose to shine its light upon it.

I began to learn to ask of that Source, that mystery, "Father, One that has birthed me, *why* am I? *Where* am I? *Who* am I?" My desire increasingly became to know the truth that could set all mankind free. I discovered that unless that freedom became fully manifest in *me*, it made no sense to talk about it with others. So I sought out the greatest of minds, the best of teachers. And yes, I was blessed by a family structure already dedicated to understanding the mysteries of what they knew as God. They led me to many such teachers.

As my own wisdom began to evolve, the teachers would look at me and say to one another,

"Something interesting is occurring here, in this son of Joseph." But there were already those who knew more about me than I knew yet about myself. Prophets, seers, astrologers and the wise ones of many cultures knew already that into the framework of the consensus mind of mankind, which you call collective consciousness, there was to be dropped a pebble, into that still clear pool, that would create ripples that would begin to change how the consciousness of humankind perceived itself.

I did not yet know these things for myself, for my very birth into this world was veiled in mystery for me, just as your birth was veiled in mystery for you as you took on being human.

As I grew, I began to have revealed to me in the depth of my silent prayer and in the depth of my very silent meditation, glimmers, insights, recognitions, and remembrances of other dimensions. I began to develop the ability to be in communication with masters of my lineage who had long since left the planet. I began to understand that consciousness is not limited to the space and volume of a body at all.

LESSON 10: *The Way Is Easy and Without Effort*

As I watched the people in their busy work, I began to see that the vast majority of beings totally confused *themselves* with the *body*. They lived as if they dwelt within the body and, therefore, were imprisoned in some strange way. They lived as if what occurred to the body occurred to *them*. They lived as if they did not know that they could transcend the body at any moment; that they could taste the vast expanse of consciousness, that they could journey to other times and places with little more than a surrendering of attention to the world they had made.

At first, I did not understand these things and I perceived myself to be quite odd. Within me, there were conflicts as the fears in my consciousness arose, the fears that are part of the human consensus reality: "Shall I remain like everyone else? Perhaps I should return to my father's carpentry shop and simply accept that I am destined to just be a carpenter."

But there were other voices that spoke to me and called me, that would come often in the night. As I developed my ability to discern these other realities, these other dimensions, by shifting my attention from the world of the body to the world of inner vision, often they would come in the night and stand beside my bed. I came to know who they were. I came to recognize the masters and teachers of a very ancient lineage of which I was a part. They would come and whisper to me:

> Forget not the purpose for which you are sent forth from the Mind of God, for through you there shall be birthed the beginning of an ancient remembrance. And your life shall become that which demonstrates to many the truth that only Love is real.

The point of all of this is simple. I want to convey to you, yet again, that the life I lived as a man was not unlike your very own. I began veiled in mystery, a child among children, a human being struggling to make sense of his world. Yes, there was within me something calling, a longing to know something that the world did not seem to teach. But is it not true that many of you have felt that same call, that same longing—to touch what is invisible, to see what cannot be seen, to hear what ears have never heard, to embrace what arms cannot reach, to abide in perfect peace and perfect trust?

LESSON 10: *The Way Is Easy and Without Effort*

Beloved friends, understand well. I say to you yet again, I come only as your brother and your friend—one who has walked as you walk, one who has breathed as you breathe, one who has cried as you cry, one who has laughed as you laugh. I am as you are.

If there be anything that I can give unto you, it is simply this: As you look upon your life and every event that unfolds within it, every time you feel that you have failed, every time that you become conflicted, every time you are sure that you will never be able to transcend all of these ups and downs and emotional waves that seem to come with living in your world, remember, I have overcome the world. And because I have done it, it is done for you, already.

Why? Because we share the same infinite field of Mind that far transcends all levels and dimensions of manifestation. You can tap into what has already occurred. You need only look upon me as your brother and friend, and *acknowledge* that the world has been overcome, and then accept the freedom, which is the effect of its overcoming, *as your own*.

So that you learn to sit in your chair, after your five minutes of abiding as Christ, in which you say to yourself:

> Here, I am free.
> Heaven is now.
> The past is passed away, and I choose anew.
> This day, I commit myself to teaching only Love by sharing only loving thoughts.
> This one day, I will look upon each one that comes into my experience and I will first breathe deeply the presence of the Holy Spirit.
> And I will look out through eyes transformed by the simple acknowledgment of the truth: All minds are joined, and I see not a stranger before me, but one who walks as I walk, who feels as I feel, who longs as I long, who is humbled as I am humbled, who prays for peace as I have prayed.
> Therefore, I will give them what they seek. And in that giving, I receive it.

Acknowledge the Truth That Sets You Free

The way is so simple and so easy that the mind of the world overlooks it, thinking that it simply

Lesson 10: *The Way Is Easy and Without Effort*

cannot be. But that which is simple seems impossible to that which insists on complexity. And a mind that insists on conflict simply cannot accept that there *is* another way. Yet what waits before you is simply this: In the end of all of your struggles, in the end of all of your doubts, and in the end of all of the moments of your unconscious conforming to the mind of the world, there remains the simple choice to be made—the choice to acknowledge the truth that has *already* set you free:

> I and my Father are one. It has been that way forever.
>
> It was accomplished in the being of Jeshua ben Joseph, who revealed to me the truth of myself, because he loved me. And if he can do it, I can do it. Even in this moment, I accept my destiny to walk this Earth awake and at peace, in mastery, and not in fear. And I begin my ministry now.

For who can you seek that can heal you? Who can you discover that can bring some form of magic to you that can overcome your resistance to the Truth? Look high and low and you will not find them. Seek forever, and you will remain a seeker forever. For the Truth is set within your heart and all power under Heaven and Earth is given unto you. It is *that* power that changes the momentum of the mind and heals every wounded perception.

In the end of all seeking, you must look into the mirror and decide to be the one who heals yourself. *You* are the one who decides, from infinite freedom, how to use the power of your mind in each moment. Therefore, the only question that a seeker of truth really truly need ask him or her self is this:

> Would I know conflict or peace? Would I be right or happy?
> Would I see the complete neutrality of all events in this world as wisps of a dream, being birthed and passing away?
> Would I see myself whole and complete?
> For as I look upon the world, I have judged myself. And as I look upon myself, I judge the world.

This was the simple secret that I once discovered when I walked upon your planet. It was not about achieving some grand mystical state of consciousness. It was not about acquiring great powers that

Lesson 10: *The Way Is Easy and Without Effort*

could attract the attention of thousands. It was not even about being able to manifest, although these powers may indeed often express themselves through the mind as it awakens.

It is about accepting the Truth that is true always, and being determined to allow that Truth to be the foundation from which you *enjoin* each and every moment of your experience.

> I am awake. I am safe. I am at peace.
> What do I truly want this moment to be for?
> For as I decree it, so shall it be.

Beloved friends, the way *is* easy and without effort. You exist to extend your treasure. And your treasure is that which is laid up in Heaven through the decision to remember only your loving thoughts, to extend only loving thoughts, and to allow your actions to express or to manifest in the field of time the good, the beautiful, and the holy. *Never* is your freedom taken from you. Never in any circumstance do you lose the innocent freedom to teach only Love, to be the presence of peace, to recognize that the world can give you nothing, just as the world can take nothing from you.

The Way of the Heart

When a child goes through a shift of awareness, they come to a point in their maturation process, not by struggle, not by design, not by much processing, and not by any manner of strategies. The child merely, in an instant, looks at the toys that he has been playing with and simply transcends them. The parents come home and the child has taken the toy truck and put it away in the closet. The doll is put on the windowsill and a book is picked up instead. Who makes the change? Not anyone outside that child.

When you put aside any negative habit as you would perceive it to be, when you have given up placing value in something that no longer serves you, you merely transcend it, and it is done with. No big deal. No one does it for you, you simply decide. You pull back the *value* you had placed on it, and the objects that were the symbols of what you were *valuing* merely drop out of your life.

In just this way, unenlightenment can be put away as though it were a toy that you have outgrown—by merely looking at all of the effects of unenlightenment, and then asking the question, "Is this what I wish to have continue as my experience? Or am I willing to put the doll on the windowsill, and pick up a book instead?" A book that speaks of Life, a book that is filled with wisdom, a book that teaches you how to step lightly in the world, to be in the world but not of it.

That book is the depth of your consciousness in which all things are already written. And that depth finds its source in your heart. You enter it through forgiveness, through the process of *relinquishing* the world—not hating the world, not despising the world, but simply relinquishing it. You *allow* your time to serve you in the process of relinquishing what does not serve you any longer, and what only disturbs your peace.

Commit to Awakening to the Peace Already Within You

As you cultivate that practice, you will find that the peace that is already within you, that you have touched a thousand times in a million different ways, begins to grow more constant—like the rays of the sun beginning to filter through the fog that has settled into the mountain valley obscuring the clarity of all things. Your peace descends gently, like a dove, descending as some would say, through the crown of the head, down through the brain-mind, and down even to the heart, the abdomen, and throughout the cells of the body, while the body lasts.

Gently relinquishing the world rests on your decision to choose to teach only Love, because you have realized that when you do not, the effect that you know immediately is painful, conflicted, unfulfilling, and that that is what you no longer want.

Here, you have begun to transcend the world that you have made and to reclaim the world made for you, a world that rests in perfect union, in the union of Father and son, God and offspring, Creator and created. The way *is* easy and without effort.

What value have you ever placed upon the world that has restored to you the peace that you seek? You have mistakenly thought, "Oh, this automobile will do it; this relationship will do it; this new career will do it. If only I can take a trip to the far corners of the world, *then* I will be at peace." And so peace never quite comes.

A creator, abiding in enlightenment, knows that all events are neutral, so neutral that they have

LESSON 10: *The Way Is Easy and Without Effort*

no effect, except for those who choose to be caught up in illusions. The creator, awakened, merely creates out of devotion to the mystery of That which has created him or her. The mind of an enlightened creator does not arise in the morning and say, "How can I survive yet another day in this world?" In the morning, when an enlightened creator arises, the question is:

> How this day might I extend the treasure of the good, the holy, and the beautiful?
>
> How can I, right where I am, experience these treasures even within the space and volume of this body?
>
> How can I look lovingly upon what my physical eyes show me, so that I discern or extract the good, the holy, and the beautiful, and therefore, give them to myself?

The mind of an enlightened creator *knows* that of themselves, they do nothing. But in each moment of decision, they can *allow* the great power and mystery of Love to direct their course. They can utilize time to refine their ability to hear *only* the voice for Love, moment by moment, breath by breath, day by day, until time is translated into eternity. And the mind rests, reclines, in its perfect union with God.

Events still occur. The world is still what the world will choose to be, unaware that there walks in its midst one who is awake, who needs to make no show. They merely *are* the presence of wakefulness, knowing that in each moment they will now be *in*formed by the guidance of the Comforter, the guidance of right-mindedness, the guidance of enlightenment. So that they are no longer attached to fearing, "What should I say? What should I do? How will this person take it? How will that person take it?" The world is no longer a concern.

They experience their very life as an ongoing flowing mystery, as though something else were living through them. This is the meaning of my friend's words, "Let that *Mind* be in you which was in our Lord, Christ Jesus," as you would read in your Bible. That *Mind* is the Mind of perfect freedom. It does not belong to anyone, but it can be cultivated to flow through you.

But only—*only*—if every fiber of your beingness is wholly committed to holiness. You cannot

Lesson 10: *The Way Is Easy and Without Effort*

leave a finger outside and get to Heaven. *All* of your mind, *all* of your energy, *all* of your gifts, *all* of your very awareness must become committed to being the presence of peace. *This* is what no one can do for you. Sitting at the feet of enlightened teachers will not do it *for* you.

The wisest of students are those that hear the word and put it into practice, diligently, *for themselves*—not for their mother, not for their father, not for their spouse, not for their brother, not for their sister, not for the sake of the planet, not for the sake of the universe, not for the sake of the new dawn that is coming, not for the sake of anything but themselves. For their Self is what God created. And that Self calls out to you to honor it, by separating your Self from the illusions that you have allowed to make a home in your mind, and becoming wholly committed to teaching only Love.

There is no other way. Yes, you can learn to sit in meditation and allow the mind and body to float free, to relax. Yes, you can learn rituals that help to focus your attention so that you remember what you are committed to, and the distractions of the world do not seem to quite catch you or hook you as much. There are many strategies that you can enjoy and experience. But in the end, it is only this: a quiet choice within that no one recognizes, that no one sees, that no one hears.

This is why I once shouted at the Pharisees, "Oh yes, you indeed get your reward standing on the street corners letting everybody know that you are fasting and praying, when you should go into your own closet to pray." That is, to be in your own privacy, making not a show, but simply using each moment to reaffirm your commitment to learning all that Love is by teaching it. By the word teach, I mean simply that you choose to express only Love in each moment.

Forgiveness is an act through which you learn what Love is, that carries you into a transcendence of the world. Sharing only loving thoughts—supportive thoughts—as you look gently upon the Christ in another is a way that takes you into the transcendence of the world. Looking upon all things of this world and seeing their perfect harmlessness, their lack of ability to constrain you or imprison you, is a way that takes you beyond the world.

Lesson 10: *The Way Is Easy and Without Effort*

And yet all of these things rest on the practice of "seeking first the Kingdom," which means not to believe in me, not to have some theological notion about what God is, not to adhere to a certain religion, or a certain church doctrine. *The Kingdom of Heaven is within you.* It is the very power of choice. Which pebble will you drop into the pool of your consciousness?

Imagine reaching a point where, just prior to every action that you engage—without ritual, without difficulty, without the grand shows and displays, the burning of incense and the lighting of forty million candles and all of the Gregorian chants or the rock and roll or whatever you choose, without *any* of it—in the silent temple of your heart, you make a simple choice:

> In this moment, I am going to discover
> what it means to teach only Love.

It might be a simple smile. It might be to let your eyes gaze at the beauty of a flower, and say, "Ah, it is very good." It might be to eat your breakfast and actually *be* there while you are eating it, instead of letting your mind run off to the office.

Here, beloved friends, is the way to the Truth

that sets you free. You must absolutely become wholly committed to being awake for no other reason than that you have realized you have no other choice. You have already made them all and they have only led to pain.

Recognizing the Presence of Christ Within

Your Self is calling out to be recognized for what it is—an awakened master, the presence of Christ in you that would inform every step, inform every decision, inform the quality of your perception, inform the very nature of your forever-expanding, transparent consciousness. For it is your consciousness, alone, that can reach out and embrace all created things, until you literally realize that all things have arisen from within you!

That is how *big* you are! That is how *grand* you are! Why? Because that is *all* you are! You are the ocean from which waves and waves of dimensions and worlds have arisen. *That Mind* is what you are required to let be in you, even as once it was within me, as I walked upon your Earth. Do not make it difficult.

Lesson 10: *The Way Is Easy and Without Effort*

Whenever you hear of a teacher teaching this or a teacher teaching that, ask yourself this: Do they offer me simplicity or complexity? Do they offer an ordinary peace, or must I have several trappings around me? Do they give me complex meditations and prayers and things to do, or do they simply remind me of the Truth and ask me to rest in it? Will they tell me that I need to go on a thousand pilgrimages? Or do they remind me that when I make my cup of tea in the morning, Heaven is present, if I will remember who is making the tea? Christ is.

Be, therefore, not distracted. For in the end of this age, there is coming forth a whole smorgasbord of those who profess to be teachers of enlightenment who will guide you into all knowledge. Look carefully, do they demand of you that you follow them? Do they demand of you that you give up your own discernment?

Or do they ask you to look deeper within? Do they ask you, "What are *you* feeling? What do *you* think? What do *you* want to do? Are *you* willing to accept responsibility for the effect? What do *you* believe? What do *you* want? You are free. I am equal to you. I am just in the role of a temporary guide for you and someday you will be far beyond me."

How do they speak? What do they teach? Is their fear filtering into their words? Do they believe that they must teach you to control the forces of nature, the forces of the mind? Do they teach you to protect yourself against evil? There are many who profess to be teachers of enlightenment, and there will be many more. When you hear these things coming from them, turn and flee from their presence! For you do not need them. You are already beyond them.

Ask only:

>   How can I extend my treasure this day?

And lay up treasures where moth and dust cannot corrupt, that is, where time, materiality, the body and the world cannot "hook you." Rather lay up treasures that are in Heaven: forgiveness, peace, unlimitedness, recognition of your unlimited power, that which brings you joy and puts a smile upon your countenance. Lay up for yourself these treasures and all things shall be added unto you.

For there is a way of being in the world that

LESSON 10: *The Way Is Easy and Without Effort*

requires no planning or striving, though to enter it does require the relinquishing of fear. To enter it requires a commitment to teaching only Love, until the mind is again whole and undivided.

There is a way of being in the world that is not here at all. The body still abides. Yes, you still act just like everybody thinks you act. That is, they know your name; they know where you live. You know which car you are supposed to drive; you know whom you go home to at night. But through it all, there is pervaded in your consciousness a transparency as you look upon all things.

Whatever feelings arise, come and go. But somehow you begin to recognize that you are much larger than the things that come and go, that you are watching a dance of shadows, a dream, gently passing by, that is gone in a cosmic split second. This does not become a way in which you *deny* your experience. Rather, it gives you the freedom to embrace it and live it totally, with passion, with purpose, with power, and in perfect freedom—no anxiety, no pressure, just the willingness to dance in the world of dreams, while remaining awake.

If, indeed, you have been putting your five minutes into practice, you are already carrying yourself closer and closer, or perhaps more and more deeply, into the transparency I am describing for you.

And that transparency grows to a point—you might think of it as a critical mass—when suddenly you as a beingness can no longer even hold the thought of yourself as a body in space and time. Then the body simply dissolves away, and your consciousness will never experience the limitations of the body again. But you will bring the joys that bodily experience taught you with you, for they are imprinted in your consciousness forever.

This Earth is a beautiful place, but it is only a pale reflection of the radiant, transcendent beauty of the good and the holy that pervades my Father's creation. Love it, embrace it, thank it, but do not cling to it.

Learn, then, to teach only Love.

A Simple Practice

Now, to build on what you have been doing, we would simply ask you to add this very simple

LESSON 10: *The Way Is Easy and Without Effort*

practice. When you sit in your chair for five minutes abiding as Christ, remembering the Truth that has set you free, begin to ask yourself the simple question:

> This day, how can I extend my treasure?
> How can I add to that which I am storing up in the Heaven of my consciousness?

Immediately, you will begin to get pictures—an old friend who needs a phone call, someone to write a letter to. It could be something as simple as picking up your cat, placing it upon your lap, and seeing all of infinity in that living being, and feeling the joy that comes as you run your hand along its fur. It could be something as grand as going to Washington, D.C. in order to send a blessing to your president. It does not matter what it is because that voice of Love will be guiding your actions. It may be as simple as turning to your spouse and saying, "You know, I appreciate you."

Whatever it is, let the day not fade away until that action is accomplished, or at least set into motion.

So the great question is:

> Am I willing to trust the flow from My

Father's Mind, through my own, as that which empowers me to extend my treasure? Yes, it does mean living unlike the way the world lives. Yes, it does mean going against the grain. You may seem to need to apply more energy to it at first, as you get the momentum of your mind to turn in another direction, to shake loose all of the sludge that has settled into your consciousness.

But I can promise you, if you will take up such a path—simply, joyfully, gently, patiently—*the end of your journey is certain.* If you choose a path filled with magic and many complex strategies, the end is not so certain. The way is easy and without effort:

> I am already That which I seek.
> I need only allow it to guide me.
> While this body lasts, I will allow it to be a
>   communication device that extends the
> treasure of perfect Love, perfect safety, and
>   perfect peace to all who enter my house.

And your *house* is your field of energy, the expanse of your presence.

Toward the end of your five minutes, look at yourself from within your mind's eye, as though from the day you began this course until now, you have journeyed around a circle.

You have journeyed through many influences of energy. You have engaged yourself in relationship with countless brothers and sisters. You have had thousands of visions and dreams and revelations come to your consciousness. You have had umpteen million opportunities to be disturbed and lose your peace. You have been like a sojourner, the prodigal son or daughter who has gone out through the realms of human consciousness and *now* you see yourself completing the circle.

Celebrate Your Re-birth as Christ

Count the days, from this day until the twenty-fifth of December. Or if you are reading these words at another time of year, simply choose a date—approximately seven weeks in the future—signifying for you *your* day of re-birth.

Let each day be seen as a step, a pilgrimage, a completion of a very ancient circle. Let each day be one in which you reaffirm your commitment to releasing everything unlike Love in yourself, so that as you come to December twenty-fifth or your appointed day, you will dedicate yourself to being prepared for it.

On December twenty-fourth or the eve of your chosen day, go to bed early enough, and in quiet and in prayer, so that you can awaken before the first rays of the new day come to caress the Earth.

Take yourself outdoors, even if you must bundle up the body. Make haste to a place of vision, a place where you can look out over wherever you live. Let that represent your ability to look out over all of creation.

There, turn to face the direction of the arising sun, and go into a simple prayer. Close your eyes. Realize that you see nothing through the physical eyes anyway. Stand with the arms at the sides and the palms open. Breathe deeply into the body, relax the mind, and begin simply to say within yourself:

> Death has occurred, and now the birth of
> Christ is at hand. Father, I accept fully
> your will for me. Your will is only that I be
> happy and use time to extend my treasure.
> Now, I receive the warmth of your Light
> and your Love.

Lesson 10: *The Way Is Easy and Without Effort*

Then, merely stand and wait, and receive the warmth of the light. For rest assured, even if the skies are cloudy, as the sun arises, there is a change in the energy of the air. If you are quiet, you can feel how it begins to affect the energy sphere of your awareness and of your body. Drink that solar energy in through every cell of your body. Drink it in until you feel your very spinal column warmed.

And when the whole body—from the crown of the head to the tips of the toes and down through each finger—is filled with light, then gently open the eyes of Christ, and let yourself see a new world, a new creation, a new beginning. Now the journey *to* the Kingdom is over, and the journey *within it* can begin. Graduate school is just around the corner.

When you journey back to your home on that December twenty-fifth morning or the morning of your chosen day, do something that celebrates *your* birthday—not mine—*yours*. I can handle taking care of my own celebration. Be joyous and celebrate in whatever way you wish. And know that the new age, the new day, has dawned. Never again will you ever be able to convince yourself that there is an excuse for believing in anything that is less than an enlightened Christ consciousness.

Regardless of when you may be reading these words, the same truth applies. Choose a date, approximately seven weeks in the future, to signify *your* day of re-birth. And surrender to this process I have described each day until that day arrives.

Your instruction is given. Reflect well on what has been given, for we have been stepping into some very simple, but very powerful initiations that were once given to me as I too awakened to the reality that only Christ dwells within me.

Beloved friends, reflect well on all that has been shared. Do not take it lightly, although it is only filled with light. Consider well each phrase, each sentence, and even the spaces between the words. For in those spaces, revelations can come. It is time to birth fully the presence of the peaceful Christ within you

Peace be unto you always. And always am I with you. Amen.

Lesson 11

A Meditation Into the Heart of Christ

Join with me in this moment. Join with me in the place where alone two minds *can* join, for the body cannot bring you to where I am. Join with me in the silent place of the heart in which all wisdom already abides. Join with me then in this moment in the place prepared for us of our Creator, before time is.

Join with me by choosing *now* to allow your attention to relax from the things of the world. Allow the eyes to gently close for just a moment, as a symbol of your willingness to set aside your involvement with and your attachment to the things of this created world. Join with me by allowing the body to be set free. This requires only that you make no demands upon it. Indeed, let it settle in, as though it was becoming again the dust of the ground from which it came.

Join with me as you let your attention recede from

the world around you. Begin to notice the thoughts that seem to stream through the mind. Join with me by moving ever yet deeper, as though you were allowing your attention to settle down, down, into the heart. And as the thoughts stream through the mind, can you tell from whence they have come? Can you tell where they have gone? They arise in a moment and fade away in a moment, while *you* continue to relinquish your attachment to all things of the world.

Verily I say unto you, even the thoughts that arise and stream through the mind ceaselessly are of the world. Settle down then, abiding in the gentle quiet of the heart. You do not cause the physical heart to beat and send the blood through the body. It simply knows, and it does. You do not cause the breath to flow through the body. It arises and passes away. It does not require your attention.

And in this moment, is it you that keep the stars in the sky above you? Is it you that keeps your beautiful Earth spinning, hurtling through space, around and around your central sun, never deviating very much at all from the same orbit it has been in since its creation? Must you attend to

Lesson 11: *A Meditation Into the Heart of Christ*

the quiet unseen way in which the flowers outside your window are growing? Can you hear the sound of the grass as it grows?

Somewhere in this very moment, a child has been birthed. Are you aware of it? Indeed, all of creation continues to go on, an eternal dance, mystery giving birth to mystery and returning to mystery without ceasing. Yet, you simply abide in a quiet place within the sanctuary of the heart.

Join with me now in perfect peace. Join with me where alone we can remember that we are together. Give up all hope of directing yourself to me by taking thought. Join with me in the simple understanding that of yourself, you can do nothing. Join with me by surrendering into the truth of a union beyond all comprehension. Settle deeply into the quiet sanctuary of the Heart we share.

That Heart is the depth and the essence of the Creator's *only* creation. That creation is pure Mind, pure Being, pure Intelligence, the fulfillment of all wisdom, the depth of all compassion, the *certainty* of every purpose under Heaven.

Rest with me, and acknowledge that our minds are joined. As you rest, again, you might notice that thoughts seem to arise and pass away. But do you not sense them, now, as though they were coming from a place where *you* are not, as though you had sunk more deeply to a place of quiet beneath the surface upon which thoughts flow back and forth without ceasing?

Are you, then, the thoughts? No, you are not. Are you even the thinker of the thoughts? No, you are not. You are merely that quiet and that presence that observes all of creation flowing through a field of awareness that *is* the Mind of Christ. Unlimited forever are you. Unchanging forever are you. Perfectly changeless are you. We are of one substance, one Light and one Truth. Here alone does reality reside. Here alone is reality remembered. Here alone Love reigns supreme. Here alone is where you are.

In this place that is everywhere at once, and in this eternity that embraces every moment of time, what do we discover? What is it that we share? It is not a body. For bodies are limited, being temporary expressions of the coalescence of thought. It is not the body that we can share. Look yet more deeply. Is it the thoughts that still dance upon the surface far above you? No. What

Lesson 11: *A Meditation Into the Heart of Christ*

is it, then, that binds us one to another, as one another? Is it not the silence and the awareness of the One who observes the arising and passing away of all created things?

I share with you the depth of a perfect silence. I share with you wisdom supreme. I abide *as you are:* the thought of Love in form. To be in form does not mean to be a body. It means only that the Christ Mind, which is the reality of Love's existence, truly abides within each of us equally. If this were not so, you could not recognize me. When you read a word, or a sentence, or a paragraph that resonates within you as being the truth, you could not know it was so, if that Truth did not already live within you as the reality of your very existence.

Remain with me now. Heed not the call of that part of the mind that would distract you and lead you back to the illusions that comprise your world. Here, there are no mates, no careers, no loss, no gain, no pain, no suffering. Here alone, the Truth remains shimmering within you. Here is where I am. And this heart that we share is not contained within your body. Rather, the body has emerged from within the power that resides in this holy place. It has provided for you only a temporary learning experience. It will be there when you return, should you desire it.

But for now, give yourself permission to rest into the heart of all creation—the still and silent place of perfect peace. What is it that we share, if not awareness itself? For here, if anyone were to look, they would see there is no difference between you and myself. You are a shimmering field of awareness. And that same shimmering field comprises the essence of *all* that I am.

Here Is the Place of Certainty, Power and Fulfillment

Within this awareness lies the answer to every question you might choose to ask. Within this shimmering awareness is the reassurance that the end of the journey is certain. Within this shimmering awareness do you abide *at one* with all minds and every aspect of creation. Join with me here often, in remembrance of me. For this is the secret of communion—to relinquish the perception of the world in favor of the acknowledgment of Reality.

Mind reaches out forever, but it reaches only to

Lesson 11: *A Meditation Into the Heart of Christ*

itself. Therefore, every word that I share with you is already present within you. Here alone, does Love abide. There is no space for anything unlike Love. This is why every loving thought is true. For it arises not from the superficial or the surface level of the mind that generates thoughts merely in reaction to other thoughts. But Love emerges from the depth of the heart that transcends what you know to be your body and your mind, your feedback mechanism.

When you think a loving thought, you have been caressed by the touch of God. When you hear not loving thoughts within yourself, this can mean only that you have returned to the surface, and have denied the depth within you.

If you would hear only loving thoughts, simply observe where your attention is. And allow it to settle deeply into this place, beyond time, beyond the body, beyond the dream of the world. For this place—the Kingdom of Heaven within you—is vast beyond comprehension. The world you know when you take your attention to the surface of the mind is contained and embraced within this heart, like a dewdrop begins to be consumed by the ocean that receives it.

Here, beloved friends, is the place of all certainty. Here is the place of perfect power to fulfill the loving thoughts with which your Creator has caressed you. Here is the way to fulfill each loving vision. Here is the source of all wisdom upon which you can draw to recreate yourself to *be* the presence of Christ incarnate.

Here then, is the straight and narrow path that leads unto Life. For Life is beyond every concept you have ever heard, even those that I have used to communicate with you. They have been like so many fingers, pointing at the moon that shines its light gently upon you. That light lives in the depth of a silent heart. Therefore, silence is the doorway to wisdom divine.

Remain with me here. Do not think on what you read, but allow it to pour through you, knowing that the vibrations of wisdom that these words carry will leave their trace upon you, without the least bit of effort on your part. You need only be as a lover to the Mind of God—opening, allowing, receiving—taking in that which your Creator would bestow upon you.

Remain with me in the depth of this perfect

Lesson 11: *A Meditation Into the Heart of Christ*

silence. Notice how you begin to feel a gentle spaciousness, a peace descending upon you, like a gentle dove—and yet, you have done nothing. And again, should you feel your attention being pulled back to the surface of your awareness, merely choose again, and return to the quiet of the heart.

I am loved, I am loving, I am lovable forever. Let this phrase be as a stairway that descends from the world of your making to the depth of perfect peace. You need repeat it only when you notice that you have become temporarily distracted by the sights and sounds and images of the world around the body, as well as the thoughts that seem to stream and dance along the surface of the brain center.

I am loved, I am loving, I am lovable forever.

As you come to feel grounded, rooted in that deep and silent place, ask whatsoever you will and its answer shall not be hidden from you. Ask to witness my lifetime as I walked upon your Earth, and it will be shown to you. Ask to be shown the vibrational field in which you were conceived in this life; it will not be hidden from you. Ask whatever you would about a friend, who perhaps has seemed troubled of late, and the source of what is occurring within them will be gently revealed to you.

For remember that in this place, you are awareness itself, merely becoming aware of itself. That awareness, that consciousness, lives equally as the essence of each and every one whom you know and love. Your love of them is what binds you to them, in the depth of a quiet awareness.

As you descend the stairway to the quiet place of the heart, there are a few things to leave behind you. Leave behind the need to be right, the need to be supported in your illusions, the fear of rejection, abandonment, denial, and death. Leave behind every thought of what the world is and what it is for. Leave behind every thought you have ever held of everyone and everywhere.

Surrender, relinquish the world of your perceptions, and come quietly to kneel before your Creator. There, in the silent place of the heart, unattached to whatever is given you or shown you, *nothing* will be kept secret. Would you know the foundations of the world? The answer is here. Would

Lesson 11: *A Meditation Into the Heart of Christ*

you know how to best direct Love to a loved one? The answer is here. A voice will speak to you, like one crying from the wilderness. Pictures will be shown to you, feelings enlivened within you, and you will know the way to extend your treasure.

Remain with me here, for here do I abide. The only difference between us is that occasionally you believe that you abide somewhere else. When you journey up those stairs, to begin to be distracted by the thoughts on the surface of your mind and by the sensory feedback of the energy field that comprises your physical creation, I remain in our shared heart, patiently waiting for your return.

Remain with me here:

> I am loved, I am loving, and I am lovable forever. This is the Truth that sets me free—I am That I Am.
>
> My awareness knows no limitation and all worlds arise within me. I am that Mind, present in all beings when they descend the stairway and embrace the Truth that alone is true always.
>
> Here is perfect peace.

Here is the recognition that nothing is lacking.
Here is the embrace of the fulfillment of the Love I have sought in all the wrong places.
Here alone, do I abide.
Here alone, do I remain.
I am That One, existing before all worlds.
This alone is the Truth about me.

These words are not mine, they are *ours*. And we share in them, equally. I am loved, I am loving, I am lovable forever. I am That I Am.

Out of the depth of that perfect silence and the remembrance of that perfect knowledge, there comes the impulse of a loving thought:

Take Me into form. Take Me into space and time. Reveal Me to the world.

Your life can become—whenever you choose it to be so—merely the process of Christ's incarnation. Relinquish the world, even as you walk through it. Surrender it with every breath. Learn to cultivate the depth of this knowing in the midst of all activities in which the body is used as a temporary learning and teaching device.

Beloved friends, abide with me in this *union*. Regardless of what the eyes of the body show

Lesson 11: *A Meditation Into the Heart of Christ*

you, regardless of what the ears of the body hear, regardless of the "harmless" thoughts that seem to dance across the surface of the brain-mind, you abide where I am, in-formed by that Love from which there has been birthed the sun, the moon, and all of the stars of Heaven, the planets in their orbits, and all dimensions within our Father's creation.

You can realize the incarnation of Christ by coming to dwell in the Heart of Christ, until every step, every word, and every gesture flows from this deep and silent and perfect place, until *its* voice is the only one upon which you act.

Even as the thoughts of the world stream through your brain-mind, even as the sensory data are received through the cellular structures of the nervous system of the body, you can relinquish these things, and act only from that depth of perfect wisdom, perfect safety and perfect peace. Let this be a time of "thanksgiving." Will it be that time in which you truly give thanks for the grace that sets you free? Will you honor that grace by descending the stairway to the quiet places of the heart in each of your days?

I am loved, I am loving, and I am

lovable forever.

I am That I Am: infinite awareness—birthless, deathless—that which embraces the dream of space and time, and looks lovingly upon all harmless and neutral events.

Even the body is no longer mine. It merely arises and passes away, while I, the creator of all creation, inform it with the awareness of perfect forgiveness, perfect peace, and the fulfillment of Love.

Yea, though I walk through the valleys of space and time, fear arises not within me. For all good things are in my safekeeping, stored where moth and dust cannot corrupt, where thieves cannot break in to steal.

Here alone, is the treasure that I seek no longer because I have found!

Abide here with me, until the hour comes when you know that you will go out no more from our Father's holy place. That place is this depth of peace that abides wherever you are as the very heart and essence of your reality:

> I am loved, I am loving,
> and I am lovable forever.

Lesson 11: *A Meditation Into the Heart of Christ*

This I give you as a divine meditation and way of prayer. Perfect it! Live it! Drink it in! Embrace it! Devour it! Become it! For in this becoming, you will merely *remember* what has always been true since before the arising of all worlds.

As a bird returns to rest in its nest, as the melting snow becomes a river that flows into the depth of a silent ocean, so too be you wise as serpents and dissolve into this depth of the Truth of your being often, until you abide here in every *where* and every *when*.

And when the body steps upon the Earth, the touch of the foot upon the earth will remind you of Christ's blessing. And when the vocal chords are used to form words, the words that shape themselves will teach only Love. Here then, beloved friend is the essence of all that I would extend to you in this lesson.

Now practice gently descending and ascending upon the ladder of awareness. Give yourself permission to ascend, to notice the thoughts that stream through the mind. Hear the sounds around you. Feel the weight of the body in the chair where you sit, and then descend again.

Abide a little while.

Then again choose to ascend. Listen to the sounds around you, the beating of the physical heart. Shift the weight of the body. Notice the thoughts that stream through the surface of the mind. Relinquish these things, and descend again, gently ascending and descending. For as you do so, you will join both poles together. And you will cultivate within yourself the awareness and the spiritual power necessary *to be in the world, but not of the world.*

Can there be a greater accomplishment than this? Can there be anything that can offer to you a greater fulfillment than to be the conduit through which infinite awareness and power flows with every breath, every gesture, every spoken word—to reveal Christ to the world through you? What could you ever value greater than this?

Enjoy, then, your practice. Know that when you descend to that place of the silent heart within you, I will greet you and I will sit with you in the depth of that silence. And our minds and our hearts and our souls shall merge as one. When you ascend, you take me with you. And when

Lesson 11: *A Meditation Into the Heart of Christ*

you descend, you drink me into yourself, until finally there is no difference between us. When the world looks upon you, they will say:

> Behold, I am in the presence of something mysterious, something attractive, something vast and peaceful and filled with power.
> Surely, this is the Child of God!

From that Mind that we share as *one*, I say again unto you:

> May peace walk with you.
> My blessings I give unto you, not as the world gives, give I the voice for Christ that longs to be your voice.
> For the world gives and takes away, but my Love is with you forever.
> Let this Love become your very own.
> Claim it. Own it. Taste it.
> Drink it. Breathe it. Walk it. Talk it.
> Incarnate it!

Though I go now to recede into silence, yet do I walk with you on the way that you will choose, that it might become a way that extends the treasure of your perfect knowledge that you are loved, that you are loving, and that you *are* lovable forever. That you are, indeed, That which you are. And you cannot be anything else! Gently touch each moment with that which you bring from what you discover in the depth of your journey into the Heart of Christ.

Peace be with you always and light your way while yet you abide within the world. You are, indeed, sent forth as Christ who holds all power to extend the treasure of Truth. Be you, therefore, That which you are—and you are the stars that light the heavens and bring radiance to the things of time. *Go you, therefore, into all the world and bless it with the radiance of the Christ within you.*

If ever you need to know where you should be, descend to that depth. And when you ascend, open the eyes and bless the place where you are. In this is your purpose fulfilled.

Peace be unto you always. Amen.

For an audio recording of this guided meditation see the Shanti Christo website, at www.shantichristo.com.

Lesson 12

Receive the Pearls of Grace

Once again, we come forth to abide with you and to celebrate with you. Once again, we come to abide with the holy Mind that *is* the Sonship. We come to abide with our brothers and sisters, and we come *as* brothers and sisters. Indeed, we come forth to abide in that process whereby the Sonship is remembering itself as the son. Indeed, beloved friends, I come forth to share that with you that already resides within you.

I come forth—*we* come forth—to join with you who have chosen to answer a certain call to bring forth a creative expression that can signify to the world the Truth that alone can set this world free. Free of what? Free of fear and all of the children that fear begets—guilt, dishonesty, unworthiness, limitation, need for suffering, judgment, and the list goes on and on.

Ultimately, when a gardener seeks to improve

the quality of the soil from which he would want his flowers to bloom forth, the gardener seeks not to look upon the effects of a weed, or that which is above the surface. But rather, he makes haste and goes for the root. When the root has been pulled up, the effects of that weed can no more be seen.

Therefore, in truth, we come not to improve what you would be thinking of as the surface of the garden, the surface of the soil, but to strike at the root that resides deep within the mind, in the depth that I have called the heart or the soul. All that we endeavor to do, then, is designed to *up*root the weed of fear that has made a home in the depth of your being.

The Way of the Heart has been designed to bypass the cognitive or thinking mind, and to strike at the roots of fear that abide in the depth of the mind in a place that is, by and large, unconscious. *All* that we do seeks to dissolve *that root* from the depth of your being.

These first twelve lessons have required you to *truly* participate with the devotion necessary to extract the wisdom that has been offered to you.

We cannot do this *to* you; we can only do it *with* you. For never can anything be forced upon the mind of the Son of God. The Holy Spirit makes no effort to usurp, or take from you, your freedom. For in your freedom, all power under Heaven and Earth resides.

Discover the Obstacles to Love

Grace does not descend until your Father knows that you are willing to prepare a place to receive it. This is why, in the process of healing and awakening, it is not necessary to *seek* for Love. It is only necessary to prepare the place, the soil, by choosing to discover the *obstacles* to Love—which all come down to fear—and to be willing to loosen that root, that it might be removed from the garden of your consciousness.

Then, the rain of grace that purifies, transforms, awakens, and brings Christ consciousness to the mind can descend gently. For when the rain falls upon hard ground, it strikes the soil and runs off, and the garden remains barren. But the wise gardener, who has softened the soil, reached in and begun to pull up the roots, sifted the soil and made it soft, open and porous with the intent of bringing forth a beautiful garden, will, indeed, be assisted. Then, the rain of grace will fall gently, without it being earned. It is given freely.

Drops of grace have been offered to you in each and every lesson. Some you have received; some you have not noticed. Some are waiting to penetrate the deeper levels of your consciousness as you continue in your willingness to release fear. Suddenly, a pearl of grace that has not yet been received will sink deep. Then, the recognition will come; the awakening will come.

Suddenly you will find yourself saying, "Wait a minute. This insight, this vision, this realization I've just had sounds like something that was in the first lesson. I think I'll go back and have another look. Yes, there it is! I wonder why I didn't notice it the first time?" It is simply the natural process in which the drops of rain of grace had not yet a place to be received.

Understand then—and this is of great importance as we move into this next part of *The Way of Mastery*—that all that transpires from *this* point rests on how well the gardener has cultivated the soil with the tools that have been given. If they have not been utilized, the soil remains hard, and the drops of rain run off and pool in the side of the garden, waiting for the soil to be properly prepared.

Of all that has been given that can continue—and will continue—to serve you the greatest will be the simple five-minute practice of abiding as Christ. And observing all that you see, all that you feel, all that you think, as though a perfectly awakened Christ was the *only* one sitting in the chair.

I know that this sounds simplistic for you, but the way *is* easy and without effort. Complexity is born of the world, and not from the Mind of God. Therefore, continue well in that practice, and allow it to be the foundation from which the soil is prepared—the roots of fear are loosened—even in ways that you cannot comprehend with the thinking mind. For the roots of fear are not merely ideas. They are the effects of ideas. They have been allowed to penetrate deep into the unconscious.

This is why the next twelve lessons, called The Way of Transformation, requires not striving, but allowing; not thinking, but letting go into *feeling*; not doing, but trusting.

Those roots of fear must be dissolved at a level that is deeper than the conscious thinking mind can reach. The mind was never designed to be your master, but to become aligned as a servant of the awakened heart, just like the flower blooms and sends forth its scent for all to see from the depth of the soil that is unseen, but has been well prepared. So that the only roots that gather nourishment from the soil are the roots of that which speaks of Life and beauty, not that which speaks of fear and unworthiness.

Seek you, then, to seek no more. For the place is prepared for you, and you need only go *to* it. Therefore, we will be cultivating more deeply the art of surrendering, resting ever more deeply into that place of silence which is the threshold to perfect wisdom divine. The Way of the Heart is the preparation of the soil that allows The Way of Transformation to truly occur.

Transformation is not complete unless it envelops, encompasses and is expressed through the very life you know, right there on your speck of dust, whirling about one sun in a small part of one universe. Expressed on your Earth and in your time frame, your relationships, your experience and in

Lesson 12: *Receive the Pearls of Grace*

your life as you know it, as you live it, as you breathe it, as you *feel* it!

So, let the breath flow and realize that you have the freedom to go back over the previous lessons and see if there is anything that you missed. As you do that, do it from a place of Christedness:

> I am that one choosing to enter The Way of Transformation whereby human consciousness, the human lived experience, becomes the living expression, the fruit which has sprung forth from the soil in which the roots of grace, Love, and healing have been well planted.

Do this not from the perspective that you are doing something amiss. But out of the desire to be the master gardener, who brings forth that fruit which extends beauty and the scent of joy for all to receive, for all to see, for all to marvel.

Yet, that beauty that springs forth from the gardener's beautiful garden does not build up the ego of the master gardener, for a master gardener knows that he or she has only been the keeper of the soil. But the magic that brings forth the flower is not his or her possession, it is merely that which they have been given stewardship over: consciousness.

Consciousness is the gift of Life, streaming forth from the Mind of God. Your mind, then, is the soil of the garden. All awakening and all transformation occur nowhere save in that garden.

Some of you are still seeking to understand the mind by seeing it as something that is locked inside the shape of your skull, and is somehow co-habitating with what you call the gray matter of the brain. Rest assured, your mind is unlimited forever. The body that sits in the chair in your five-minute exercise is as a drop of foam being expressed at the slightest tip of one wave in an infinite ocean. That ocean is itself within the unlimited expanse of your mind. You are consciousness as such—pure Spirit!

The only question, then, is this. Are you willing to allow that drop of foam to be transformed into that which fully and always expresses only the Love of God, even though that expression is still temporary because the body has arisen in the field of time and disappears in the field of time? Are you willing to say, "What the heck!" and allow that Love to be as *fully embodied* as it is possible for it to be, for the split second that the body is in this world?

Expressing mastery is the effect of The Way of Transformation in *this* world, in *this* time, in *this* little tiny moment. Rest assured, to the degree that you turn your attention to expressing mastery, to the degree that you use time wisely to be the embodied Christ, when the body drops away and it veils from you no longer the magnificence of the *Light you are,* the light will not be blinding to you. You will not contract in fear. You will merely let this world go gently and as easily as a child has put away a toy that has been outgrown, because its usefulness is complete.

All that you see—the body, your relationships, your devices, and your stars, your winds and your waters—will eventually be put aside by you. Not out of denial, but simply out of recognizing that their usefulness is over.

Indeed beloved friends, as we come then to the completion of the first twelve lessons, look well to see that no drops of grace have been ignored. Open the heart ever more deeply. Allow those pearls, those drops of grace, to penetrate ever more deeply, not just as ideas in the thinking mind, but as *feelings* in the cells of the body.

Let it create for you a sweetness in the flow of breath, a sensitivity in the way your foot rests upon the soil of the Earth with each step. Let it begin to transform the way in which you rest your hand upon the shoulder of your brother or sister. Allow that sweetness to permeate your gaze as you look upon another—seeing the Christ within them that is growing into a beautiful flower whose scent and beauty will be as a blessing to many. There is no one among you who is not the evolving Christ. Remember always that what you *see* is what you *get*, in the same way that as you teach, you learn.

A Meditation of Release

Look well, then, and ask yourself this:

> Who do I know in my existence who I have judged, and locked into a certain box, and I have decided that is all they are?

There you will find a fruitful meditation for reflection. I would suggest that you use the next

Lesson 12: *Receive the Pearls of Grace*

thirty days to take time and use it wisely to allow the names, the images, and the faces of those that you have judged to come back to you and to say:

> You know, mother, father, ex-mate (whoever it is), I get it.
>
> I have placed you in a box and thrown away the key.
>
> You are stuck, so I have said.
>
> And now, I release you, that I might be released.

Contemplate their image. Allow the memories of the experiences you have shared with them to come back. If there are feelings, by all means, let yourself *feel* them. Gaze upon them in your mind, until you feel that sweetness that dissolves the imprisonment into which you have placed them. For as that imprisonment begins to melt, you will sense and know that your freedom is blossoming.

You cannot take fear into Love. You cannot take judgment into forgiveness. You cannot take limitation into unlimitedness. These things must be released at the level in which they were first created. Therefore, make note that this practice should not be overlooked. Give yourself thirty days with the goal to truly go back and shall we say, mop up any forgiveness or releasing that you need yet to do. Do not let the mind say, "I don't know if I did that well enough." For understand, it is the Comforter that releases you and the other, through your willingness to allow it to occur.

Now there are some effects. This will mean that when you have truly done that, never again do you have any justification or excuse for attaching any experience you have had or any feelings you have ever felt to the hook on the side of their imprisonment that you have placed them in. Often, the human mind, the egoic mind, wants to hang the coat of its judgment on the hook just outside the bars in which you have locked someone.

For instance, "That which I have experienced is the result of my father's alcoholism. That which I have experienced in life is the result of my mother having forty thousand affairs a week. That which I have experienced is the result of my business partner who has stolen my golden coins. That which has caused my suffering is the result of the position of the stars in the sky when I chose incarnation. If only *they* would have gotten it right, *I* would be fine."

Lesson 12: *Receive the Pearls of Grace*

As we conclude The Way of the Heart, I say unto you, do not enter The Way of Transformation until you have *truly* and *fully* satisfied your awareness that you are not clinging to even the subtlest iota of perception that, in any way, you are a victim of the world you see. Nothing has been caused by your relationships. All of them have merely shown you what you have already decided will be true. The world, then, is not the cause of *anything*. You merely see what you have used the freedom of your consciousness to concoct about yourself.

For example, lack is not caused by taxation. Taxation is caused by the decision to need to believe that there is a power outside of yourself that needs all of your energy. Government does not cause you to be subservient. Your sense of being subservient, guilt ridden, weak, and limited is what births the idea of government. Then some of you as loving brothers and sisters say, "Well, I'll play that part." They become your politicians that create the disgruntled feelings that you have.

The world is uncaused by anything, save the choices you have made as a free consciousness.

You have concocted the thought and then immersed yourself in that which reflects back to you what you have already decided to believe. This means that The Way of Transformation is that way in which one becomes empowered, in every moment, to become fully responsible for clearly deciding what they will see and that they will not settle for anything less. The better you get at this, the quicker it happens. Until one reaches the point where miracles occur.

Yet, they are only miraculous to those that do not understand how consciousness works. You can achieve that place in which you hold out the palm of the hand and desire the sweetest tasting apple that has ever been created, and it will, literally, appear in the palm of your hand. Of course, at that point, you will be well beyond any need whatsoever to even hold the thought of requiring physical form.

You will begin then to get a sense of your mastery by being able to look at the world you see and observe clearly what has been changing in it. You will observe how quickly and effortlessly that which the heart truly desires—because it is in alignment with the Mind of God—becomes

Lesson 12: *Receive the Pearls of Grace*

manifested, effortlessly. When the gap between the pure desire and the manifested reflection of it is smaller and smaller and smaller, you will literally sense in the feeling body that mastery is growing.

You will know that you are merely a Child of God playing, without ceasing, in the sandbox of all possibilities called the Mind. And that there is, literally, nothing out there that is solid, nothing out there that is unrelated to you.

So, that is where we are going if you wish to come along on the journey, if you are willing to truly become committed to uprooting every root of fear that has taken hold within the depth of the mind that has been rendered unconscious because of your hatred of yourself. It is called the separation from God. And therefore, because it has become unconscious, it has ruled you. Time to release the un-rule-able, by allowing that alone which can uproot the root of fear to come and take up its rightful place within you: Christ-Mindedness.

You have your homework before you, then. Go within and ask, "Have I taken the time to fully focus on each lesson?" You may realize, "When I read the third lesson, I was trying to watch the football game on television. I wonder if I missed something? When I read the seventh lesson, I was thinking about going out to dinner. Did I really sit with it and extract all of the pearls that were offered? Perhaps I will go back and really set aside some quiet time in which I deliberately put the world aside and hang on every word."

Yet, do so with a relaxed body and a soft breath and a non-grasping mind. Be you therefore like a sponge that allows the raindrops to be absorbed into the self, and that is all. Knowledge is not a cognitive struggle. It is not the arranging of ideas in some order that satisfies the thinking mind.

Knowledge is the receiving of a vibration that begins to soften the soil of the heart and dissolve the root of fear from your being. Knowledge is the result of the transformation of the garden that you have been given and entrusted with—the field of mind that is you. That mind pervades the body. It pervades the space around you and melds and dances with other infinite webs of relationship called other minds—energy dancing into energy, unlimited forever, out of which all

Lesson 12: *Receive the Pearls of Grace*

things of time are birthed and pass away.

So, you see, where I abide is everywhere at once. And so do you; you simply do not know it yet. I abide with an infinite array of friends who have *realized* the Truth and have been set free. They are infinitely creating, without ceasing, that which extends their treasure, which is the good, the holy, and the beautiful. Many have given you images of choirs of angels singing the praises of God. It is the same thing.

For when extension of joy becomes free to express only the good, the holy, and the beautiful, it is like a vibration of many notes, a choir of creative consciousness, sparks of divinity, who abide in perfect unlimitedness and *know* it. And ceaselessly extend their deepest bliss by allowing the good, the holy, and the beautiful to flow through them from the infinite, mysterious, ungraspable, uncontainable Mind that is God. Just as the sunlight of the sun creates and streams through many sunbeams that extend out to the far reaches of your universe as light, out of which planets are birthed, and animals and water and trees and birds and man.

Imagine, then, *that* is your destiny—to take up your rightful place beside me, to join your brothers and sisters in infinite and perfect creativity, like a harp player who ceaselessly runs the fingers across the strings creating the most beautiful notes. The combinations never cease.

In every moment, you experience the fruit of the flowers springing forth from the garden that you have well prepared to receive the rain of grace. The good, the holy and the beautiful flow through your unobstructed mind that rests in perfect marriage or union, with that which is your Creator, your Source, evermore, evermore, *evermore*.

Not a bad way to spend eternity! But if you look ahead, and feel that there is a distance between where you are and where that reality is, you will miss the opportunities required—right where you are—to practice where you are going, by being it *now*. You have heard it said that a journey of a thousand miles begins with the first step. And the beginning is every bit as important as the end. For in the beginning, the end is already present.

The Way of Transformation asks you to truly become present where you *are*, to deliberately

Lesson 12: *Receive the Pearls of Grace*

and consciously cultivate, with every thought and every breath, the willingness necessary that allows the root of fear to be dissolved. So that the good, and the holy, and the beautiful are *all* that emanate from you, like a beacon being sent out to creation around you.

Do not delay. Do not *waste* time. Time can, indeed, be wasted. But listen well, for time can also waste. You have a saying we would perceive in many of your silly movies, where someone gets "wasted." How many times have *you* been the one who has said to yourself, "Well, I think I'll just waste myself?" How many ways have you gone unconscious? How many ways have you numbed your feelings? How many ways have you judged your brother or sister? How many ways have you decided to hold onto thoughts such as, "I could never do that. What's the point? It's a waste." Oh, yes! You just put a gun to your head and pulled the trigger. You have wasted *yourself* by wasting time.

Every moment is as a doorway through which the good, the holy, and the beautiful can be expressed, as the cultivation of the consciousness through which the power to do so grows. Oh, beloved friends, those moments of your time are very precious! Do not look out upon the world thinking that it is just the same old world.

Remember, then, as you begin to come to the completion of the study of The Way of the Heart, that what you see *outside* of you is only the reflection of what you have allowed to live within you. And simply ask:

> Is this what I wish to continue? What do I truly want? What is this, my very consciousness for? What do I commit myself to? What do I say I believe? Where do I freely choose to place the power of valuation?

For what you value, you experience immediately. The world will bow down and say, "Very well. You have let us know what you value. We will mirror it back to you, because we love you, because we are a part of you. And heaven forbid that we would take away your free will."

So if you value hopelessness, the world will be a hopeless place. If you value lack of golden coins, you will continue to see lack of golden coins, which just means lack of a flow of energy. If you value loneliness, you will continue to be alone. If you value the right to be in judgment of another, you will experience the fruit of separation.

If you value sweetness, sweetness will come. If you value receiving Love—listen to this carefully—if you value *receiving* Love, the world will begin to show up at your doorstep in completely different embodiments. Different vibrations, different thought patterns will be mirrored back to you that let you receive Love. For nothing can be received until the place is prepared for it to enter. And you can only *give* what you have been willing to receive. If you receive a drop of water into your glass, that is all that you can give to another. But he that receives all, gives all. And he that gives all, receives tenfold more.

Call for Assistance to Dissolve Fears

The Way of the Heart is a good beginning. We have called out to you across space and time, and if you have heard the call, the connection or the relationship with us is already established. There is, then, no bridge to cross—only the willingness to receive what is true:

> Jeshua is available for me always.

Mary is available for me always.

The one you would call as my friend, St. Germain is available for you always. The entire family, lineage of masters have sought through time to create a frequency and a vibration that can dissolve the effects of the negative thinking that you have extended out of your mind, that creates the smoke and the veil around you. To dissolve that, all of us are available to you, and our number is legion!

Rest, assured, you are not alone. In any moment, you need only call upon me, and I am with you. And I do not come alone! For some of you, then, we would highly suggest that in those moments when you feel like you need a little help, when fear seems to be coming up, but you know you must go ahead, whatever it be, whatever you think you are fearing, simply say:

> Legions of angels and masters and friends, whose number is infinite beyond comprehension, you who are sent directly of God to assist me over the ditch, come now, because I declare it and I receive it.
> And therefore it *is*!

Lesson 12: *Receive the Pearls of Grace*

Then take the step that is necessary to take. It will not be your imagination. We will be with you. And the perfect end is certain. Fear is nothing more than the illusion you have chosen to value in order to experience what it is like to feel separate from Love. That is all. You merely waved your cosmic magic wand and said, "Let there be fear so I can experience it."

We love you. Beyond your present comprehension, we love you. Beyond all comprehension — even at what you might perceive to be our level of functioning—is the presence of God's Love, which we seek to merely pour forth to you, that by *giving*, we continually *receive*. The laws of consciousness work for us just like they work for you! We are just more aware of them.

That Love which God is, is incomprehensible forever! The sunbeam can never comprehend the sun. I am a sunbeam to that sun. You are a sunbeam to that sun. We are therefore made of one substance, and that substance alone sustains us throughout eternity. The greatest of joys is to surrender fully into allowing that Light to light your way without ceasing.

The Way of the Heart

She that releases the world embraces the Creator. And he that releases fear remembers Love. She that embodies forgiveness lives at peace. And he that relinquishes control knows perfect trust. The awakened Christ that has surrendered the knot of fear, called "I," rests in unlimitedness forever, in perfect communion with all of creation. And that union never ceases. It merely expands and extends as Life comes forth, creation comes forth, extending the good, the holy, and the beautiful.

A flower that blooms in the spring for a day is the good, the holy, and the beautiful. The rays of sunlight that dance upon the oceans of this world creatively sing forth the good, the holy, and the beautiful. The bird that alights upon your fence and sings its morning song has come forth from that infinite perfect sun and its notes extend the joy of the Child of God. So, too, the smile upon one of your brothers and sisters who has received a pearl of grace through *you* is creation itself, the presence of the good, the holy, and the beautiful. Every loving thought you allow to be cultivated in the garden of your own mind extends the good, the holy, and the beautiful.

Therefore, sing that song without ceasing. Be willing, as we close The Way of the Heart, to

Lesson 12: *Receive the Pearls of Grace*

celebrate your willingness to embrace with perfect deliberateness, your creativity and the power you have—the dominion over that which is planted in the soil of your mind. Prepare that soil well as you complete the first part of this course, that the pearls of grace might bring you into The Way of Transformation.

Celebrate *your* birth as those sunbeams that are expressed through the stories of the birth of Christ into the world. For me, it occurred two thousand years ago. Is it not time now for you to let that same birthing be fully completed in you?

Know that it has been our honor and our joy to abide with you. There is a whole host of beings encircling you every moment you remember that you have chosen to answer a call that can be traced to the very Mind of God, who has reached out to call His creation—*you*—back to Himself, so that you can deliberately extend Love without ceasing.

We give you Love. We hold you with perfect patience, knowing the Truth that is true alone, about you. And we will never leave you.

Peace, then, be unto you always.

The Shanti Christo Foundation

In 1994, Shanti Christo Foundation was founded as a 501 (c) 3 non-profit organization dedicated to holding a vision inspired by Jeshua ben Joseph (Jesus). That vision is incorporated into our mission, which is to awaken the Divine Self within through offering the teachings of Jeshua ben Joseph. These transformational teachings include hundreds of hours of recorded conversations and are available in CD and MP3 format.

The vision, then, inherent in our mission is the bringing of Heaven to Earth. Shanti Christo means the "Peace of the Anointed One" an awakened state which empowers you to be all you are created to be, so that our world can be blessed by the divine gifts of each and every unique, worthy and precious individual. Shanti Christo is that pure and ever present, perfectly innocent, and completely awakened vibration which is peace.

If this book has touched your heart, you will enjoy listening to the original recordings of The Way of Mastery along with the other Jeshua material.

For a complete listing of recordings by Jeshua, other related products, and to learn more about the Shanti Christo Foundation please visit our website at:

www.shantichristo.com

Shanti Christo
FOUNDATION

A partial listing of CDs available from www.shantichristo.com.

The Way of the Heart - Set One
Twelve consecutive recordings, each designed by Jeshua to build on the previous lessons, which help anchor, inspire and teach us to awaken in Christ Mind. 12 CD set.

The Way of Transformation - Set Two
The continuation of the formal lessons from Jeshua. 12 CD set.

The Way of Knowing - Set Three
The third set of formal lessons from Jeshua. 11 CD set.

The Heart of Freedom
Described as one of the most powerfully rich recordings of Jeshua's message. CD.

The Holy Instant
Originally recorded as a Christmas message in the year 2000, this is regarded as a favorite. CD.

Heaven on Earth
A four CD recording set of Jeshua's early talks on bringing Heaven to Earth. 4 CD set.

Healing Through Self Love
An uplifting offering on the importance of loving oneself. CD.

Love Heals All hings
A two recording set with a "live" audience of A Course in Miracles students. 2 CD set.

Mastering Communication
A remarkable message on how to have genuine communication. CD.

Death and Earth Changes
Jeshua addresses the "end of an ancient dream", the transition of the Earth and humanity during these times. He also answers the question, "what happens when we die?" CD.

Grace as Reality
A two recording set describing Grace as that which brings perfect Peace to those who allow it. 2 CD set.

Questions & Answers
From the original recordings of The Way of Mastery - 6 CD set. Over 40 Q&A's, taken from the original recordings of the 35 formal lessons offered by Jeshua. These were not included in The Way of Mastery book.

I desire:
Santa Fe
Completion of book publication
To Dance
Carmel swirl ice cream
Healing = Ted
On going learning